Becoming a Nation of Readers:

The Report of the Commission on Reading

prepared by Richard C. Anderson
Elfrieda H. Hiebert
Judith A. Scott
Ian A. G. Wilkinson

with contributions from members
of the Commission on Reading

The National Academy of Education • The National Institute of Education
The Center for the Study of Reading

1985

The National
Institute of
Education
U.S. Department of
Education
Washington, D.C. 20208

The work upon which this publication is based was performed
pursuant to Contract No. 400-83-0057 of the National Institute of
Education. It does not, however, necessarily reflect the views of that
agency.

Commission on Reading

Foreword

Continuing discussion across the country of policies for improving schools is sharpening recognition of the contributions of research to educational practice. As educational decision makers consider alternative approaches to school improvement, examine current practices and revise instructional programs, research on crucial elements of the educational process is invaluable. The accumulation of findings on certain essential aspects of schooling has reached a critical mass and deserves close attention. Reading and the use and comprehension of language — the most pervasive and fundamental activity in schooling — is one such area. This report fulfills a need for careful and thorough synthesis of an extensive body of findings on reading. In its pages, the leading experts present their interpretations of our current knowledge of reading and the state of the art and practice in teaching reading.

The Research Base For
Becoming A Nation Of Readers

Three broad areas of inquiry have made *Becoming a Nation of Readers* possible. Studies of human cognition in the psychology of language, linguistics, child development, and behavioral science give us a clearer picture of reading as an integration of numerous learned processes. Research on environmental influences has described the impact of various settings on reading experiences. Investigations of classroom practices, especially those stemming from studies of teaching and of test use, have been interpreted in the light of the efforts to understand the reading process and to explicate factors that shape children's experience with written language. Given the scope of these inquiries, the Commission on Reading that guided the preparation of this document, and the scholars who wrote it, have been able to synthesize a diverse, rich body of scientific information into a systematic account of beginning reading and the comprehension of language.

The Reading Process

Research on the reading process has provided fuller understanding of how children can learn the letter patterns and associated sounds in an alphabetic language such as English, the importance of fluent word recognition, and how a text's structure influences the meaning drawn from it. It has uncovered the roots of proficient reading, and described how the development of well-practiced skills in beginning reading foster comprehension of complex texts. This research often supports accepted effective practices and removes them from unnecessary debate; the findings explain and confirm the experience and intuitions of outstanding practitioners and make their methods more widely accessible. At the same time, research findings identify practices that are less useful, outmoded, or that persist in the face of evidence to the contrary.

Knowledge about the intricacies of the reading process lay to rest once and for all some of the old debates about the roles of phonics and comprehension. We now know that learning efficient word recognition and grasping meaning are companion skills from the time a child first reads. These findings also have yielded evidence that extends early research on reading and on child development. We have learned that children bring more prior knowledge and complex mental processes to reading than was thought earlier. Reading instruction should meet the challenge of building from the knowledge that children bring to the school experience, by offering the richest texts that they are able to understand. Teaching techniques and text design can be informed by new conceptions of the potential of children's minds, and at the same time recognize individual differences in language experience and in the acquisition of reading proficiency.

Environmental Influences on Reading

Reading, comprehending, and thinking with language and the printed word are cultural phenomena. The extent of their development is affected by home and family circumstances, the encouragement of basic habits and attitudes in kindergarten and the early grades, and opportunities and social support for the development of effective skills and strategies in later life. This report addresses this complexity, understanding that too often one phase or factor of the acquisition of reading ability captures popular attention and blocks appreciation of the larger sweep of reading development.

Text comprehension depends upon a reader's prior knowledge, experience and attitudes; meaning is constructed as a reader links what he reads to what he knows. We can think of literacy as an acquired proficiency. Like achieving high levels of competence in swimming or in playing a musical instrument, competence in reading requires appropriate conditions and long periods of training and practice. This report discusses the roles of early habits and motivation; the systematic teaching of foundation skills for decoding words, developing vocabulary, inferring meaning from sentences and enjoying stories; and the further development of strategies for comprehending and interpreting textbooks in various subject matters.

The parent and the home environment teach the child his or her first lessons and they are the first teacher for reading too. Acquiring sensitivity to the sounds and rhythm of words and their meanings, a love of books and an ease of oral communication does not happen spontaneously; we can shape our homes to enable our children to become lovers of words and books. Formal school instruction takes on added value when programs in institutions out of school, like libraries, television, and museums, display attention to high standards of literacy.

Teaching Techniques, Tools, and Testing

In teaching, as in other professions, well-researched methods and tools are essential. This report makes clear the key role of teachers' professional knowledge. Research on instructional pacing and grouping and on adaptation to children's accomplishments has contributed to new ideas that can help all children master the basics and then attain levels of literacy far beyond the basic competencies. The reading teacher's repertoire must draw upon the deepening knowledge of child development, of the nature of language and linguistics, of the structure of stories that give rise to comprehension, of the art and elegance of children's literature, and of the psychology of learning. With such knowledge assisting their practices, they can best foster the acquisition of foundation skills and higher processes of comprehension. The report indicates why changes in teacher training, internship experiences, continuing education, and sabbatical periods are necessary if teachers are to learn and refine their skills for their complex task.

Becoming a Nation of Readers also draws on knowledge that has been obtained about the design of primers, workbooks and self-study lessons, the structure of stories and texts that encourage effective habits of comprehension and thinking with language, and tests that significantly drive what is taught and learned. Fruitful directions are indicated for the designers and publishers of these materials. The report goes further and points out that our understanding of reading in the context of the subject matters of schooling, science, mathematics, social studies, and literature must be carefully researched so that texts and teaching materials can be designed for effective levels of comprehension and problem solving.

The ways in which reading achievement is tested and evaluated greatly influence what is taught and the reading skills that are valued and learned. Testing is a very useful aspect of teaching and learning, but should not emphasize only the competencies that are easy to measure and thus fix our sights below essential processes. Mastery tests must not treat reading as a set of discrete skills, when research has indicated that a closely integrated set of processes supports fluent reading. The nationally normed tests used by school systems may not accommodate the expanding view of literacy this society requires. Because of our greater understanding of reading and social influences upon it, improved forms of assessment are now feasible and can supplement strengthened instructional practices and tools in raising the national levels of literacy.

With growing recognition of the contributions of research to educational practice, educational policymaking can proceed with new vigor. Issues of educational practice, like those of health care, are of pervasive concern in this society. Where sound information on topics of national concern exist, informed policymakers, professionals, and an informed citizenry can work together to assure that high standards are observed.

The Sponsorship of the Report

Becoming a Nation of Readers was produced under the auspices of the National Academy of Education's Commission on Education and Public Policy, with the sponsorship of the National Institute of Education. The Academy established this Commission in 1983 to bring its members' cross-disciplinary knowledge of research in education to bear in identifying bodies of research that might inform educational policy. This report reflects the Academy's charge that the Commission "locate topics on which there has been appreciable research and scholarship . . . and gather panels of experts from within the Academy and elsewhere to survey, interpret and synthesize research findings." With this objective in mind, the Academy called upon experts on various aspects of reading to form the Commission on Reading, chaired by Richard C. Anderson, to prepare this report.

The last two decades of research and scholarship on reading, building on the past, have produced an array of information which is unparalleled in its understanding of the underlying processes in the comprehension of language. Although reading abilities and disabilities require further investigation, present knowledge, combined with the centrality of literacy in the educational process, make the report cause for optimism. Gains from reading research demonstrate the power of new spectra of research findings and methodologies to account for the cognitive activities entailed in school learning. And because, in the schools and classrooms across the country, reading is an essential tool for success, we can hope for significant advances in academic achievement as the policies and practices outlined in these pages become more widespread.

In this effort, the Academy's Commission on Education and Public Policy and the Commission on Reading, which guided the project, have had the good fortune to engage in work that can secure greater reliability in instruction and render educational outcomes more predictably beneficial.

Robert Glaser
President
National Academy of Education

Contents

The knowledge is now available to make worthwhile improvements in reading throughout the United States. If the practices seen in the classrooms of the best teachers in the best schools could be introduced everywhere, improvements in reading would be dramatic.

Introduction

Becoming a Nation of Readers

Reading is a basic life skill. It is a cornerstone for a child's success in school and, indeed, throughout life. Without the ability to read well, opportunities for personal fulfillment and job success inevitably will be lost.

Reading is important for the society as well as the individual. Economics research has established that schooling is an investment that forms human capital — that is, knowledge, skill, and problem-solving ability that have enduring value. While a country receives a good return on investment in education at all levels from nursery school and kindergarten through college, the research reveals that the returns are highest from the early years of schooling when children are first learning to read.[1] The Commission on Excellence warned of the risk for America from shortcomings in secondary education.[2] Yet the early years set the stage for later learning. Without the ability to read, excellence in high school and beyond is unattainable.[3]

How well do American children and youth read? How well do American schools teach reading? These are difficult questions to answer objectively. Partial answers can be gleaned from historical trends in achievement test data. Studies dating back to the middle of the 19th

1

century usually have shown that succeeding generations of students perform better than earlier generations.[4] In one study, for example, 31,000 students in grades 2-6 representative of the United States at large were given a reading test in 1957 and the scores were compared to those of 107,000 students who had taken the same test in 1937. After adjusting for the fact that the 1937 sample was older by 4 to 6 months, because fewer children were promoted to the next grade at that time, the investigator concluded that children in 1957 had a reading ability advanced a half year over children of the same age and intelligence 20 years before.[5]

Recent trends in test scores are mixed. With respect to basic reading skill, as gauged by ability to comprehend everyday reading material, results from the National Assessment of Educational Progress confirm that slight gains continued to be made during the 1970s.[6] The largest gains were made by black children living in large cities. Probably these gains are attributable to the increasing aspirations and confidence of blacks and improvements in the quality of instruction that black children receive.

On the other hand, scores on tests that gauge advanced reading skill, among other abilities, showed small but steady declines from the early 1960s until the late '70s, at which point they leveled off and started to climb slightly. Declines were sharpest on the SAT and ACT, which are taken by high school seniors hoping to enter selective colleges and universities, but there were also declines on advanced tests given to all kinds of students in junior and senior high school.[7] Reasons offered to explain the test score decline include erosion of educational standards, increases in TV viewing, changes in the size of families and spacing of children, shifts in young people's motivations and life goals, and the fact that larger numbers of youth from less advantaged families have been staying in school and taking the tests.[8]

Another approach to evaluating the level of reading proficiency attained in this country is to compare our achievement with achievement in other countries. A survey of reading performance in 15 countries completed just over a decade ago showed that American students were never in first or second place on any test, and that on most tests they ranked at or below the international average.[9] A more recent comparison between the United States, Taiwan, and Japan showed a much wider spread of achievement among children in this country; many American children did well, but disproportionate numbers were among the poorest readers in the three countries.[10] International comparisons are tricky, depending, for instance, on the numbers of children in each age group that remain in school in different countries and the assumption that test items translated into different languages are really equivalent. Still, the figures offer no grounds for complacency.

How Americans have compared in the past is less urgent than the question of whether current generations will be literate enough to meet the demands of the future. The world is moving into a technological-information age in which full participation in education, science, business, industry, and the professions requires increasing levels of literacy. What was a satisfactory level of literacy in 1950 probably will be marginal by the year 2000.[11]

There is reason to be optimistic about the potential for the improvement of literacy in this country. From research supported by the National Institute of Education, and to some extent other government agencies and private foundations, the last decade has witnessed unprecedented advances in knowledge about the basic processes involved in reading, teaching, and learning. The knowledge is now available to make worthwhile improvements in reading throughout the United States. If the practices seen in the classrooms of the best teachers in the best schools could be introduced everywhere, the improvements would be dramatic.

The purpose of this report is to summarize the knowledge acquired from research and to draw implications for reading instruction. The report is intended to reach a wide audience, including the serious layman. Thus, current practices are described in some detail and a little is said about their history and rationale.

3

Based on best available information, problems with current practices are identified and the evidence and arguments for possible solutions sketched. While the report is based on research, the heavy trappings of scholarship are eschewed insofar as that is possible without diluting the message.

Based on what we now know, it is incorrect to suppose that there is a simple or single step which, if taken correctly, will immediately allow a child to read. Becoming a skilled reader is a journey that involves many steps. Similarly, it is unrealistic to anticipate that some one critical feature of instruction will be discovered which, if in place, will assure rapid progress in reading. Quality instruction involves many elements. Strengthening any one element yields small gains. For large gains, many elements must be in place.

The new knowledge about reading and schooling contains some surprises, but more often it confirms old beliefs. It answers some questions that have puzzled parents and educators, but it leaves others unanswered and sometimes furnishes conflicting answers. While there is more consensus about reading than in the past, there are still important issues about which reasonable people disagree. That knowledge about reading is incomplete is inevitable considering the marvelous complexity of the human mind and the still modest — but growing — power of social science concepts and methods.

Based on what we now know, it is incorrect to suppose that there is a simple or single step which, if taken correctly, will immediately allow a child to read. Becoming a skilled reader is a journey that involves many steps. Strengthening any one element yields small gains. For large gains, many elements must be in place.

Reading is the process of constructing meaning from written texts. It is a complex skill requiring the coordination of a number of interrelated sources of information.

What Is Reading?

Substantial advances in understanding the process of reading have been made in the last decade. The majority of scholars in the field now agree on the nature of reading: Reading is the process of constructing meaning from written texts. It is a complex skill requiring the coordination of a number of interrelated sources of information.

Reading can be compared to the performance of a symphony orchestra. This analogy illustrates three points. First, like the performance of a symphony, reading is a holistic act. In other words, while reading can be analyzed into subskills such as discriminating letters and identifying words, performing the subskills one at a time does not constitute reading. Reading can be said to take place only when the parts are put together in a smooth, integrated performance. Second, success in reading comes from practice over long periods of time, like skill in playing musical instruments. Indeed, it is a lifelong endeavor. Third, as with a musical score, there may be more than one interpretation of a text. The interpretation depends upon the background of the reader, the purpose for reading, and the context in which reading occurs.

How does the process of reading occur? A common

view is that reading is a process in which the pronunciation of words gives access to their meanings; the meanings of the words add together to form the meanings of clauses and sentences; and the meanings of sentences combine to produce the meanings of paragraphs. In this conception, readers are viewed as always 'starting at the bottom' — identifying letters — and then working up through words and sentences to higher levels until they finally understand the meaning of the text.

However, research establishes that the foregoing view of reading is only partly correct. In addition to obtaining information from the letters and words in a text, reading involves selecting and using knowledge about people, places, and things, and knowledge about texts and their organization. A text is not so much a vessel containing meaning as it is a source of partial information that enables the reader to use already-possessed knowledge to determine the intended meaning.

Reading is a process in which information from the text and the knowledge possessed by the reader act together to produce meaning. Some aspects of this interaction can be illustrated with the following passage:

> When Mary arrived at the restaurant, the woman
> at the door greeted her and checked for her name.
> A few minutes later, Mary was escorted to her chair
> and was shown the day's menu. The attendant was
> helpful but brusque, almost to the point of being
> rude. Later, she paid the woman at the door and
> left.[1]

The first phrase will lead readers to expect that their existing knowledge of restaurants will be relevant. That is to say, the word "restaurant" brings to mind past associations and experiences with restaurants and the interrelations among these ideas. From there, reading is easy because of the expectations that come from this knowledge. The woman at the door is taken to be the hostess. Mary must sit at a chair at a dining table before she can eat. The "attendant" is probably the waiter or waitress, and the person referred to as leaving in the last sentence is probably Mary. These are all inferences

8

hat make use of both the information presented in the text and the knowledge the reader already has about restaurants.

Good readers skillfully integrate information in the text with what they already know. However, immature readers may depend too much on either letter by letter and word by word analysis or too much on the knowledge they already have about the topic.[2]

Some children laboriously work their way through texts word by word, or even letter by letter (e.g. m-m-M-a-r-y). They are so intent on saying the words right that they miss aspects of the meaning. In oral reading, these children tend to make nonsensical errors that look or sound like the words they are trying to read with results such as, "The woman at the door *grated* her and *locked* for her name."[3] These children sometimes fail to use the knowledge they may have about the topic to think about what they are trying to read.

Other immature readers show an overreliance on the knowledge they already have about the topic. Such children may use pictures, titles, their imagination, and only a small amount of information in the text to produce a believable story.[4] For example, "... and then Mary got to the ... ah ... pizza place. She went in the door and greeted her friend. Then she sat down in her chair and had a pizza." These children often do not have enough skill at word identification to make use of all of the information in the written message.

Five generalizations flow from the research of the past decade on the nature of reading:

The first generalization is that *reading is a constructive process.* No text is completely self-explanatory. In interpreting a text, readers draw on their store of knowledge about the topic of the text. Readers use this prior knowledge to fill in gaps in the message and to integrate the different pieces of information in the message. That is to say, readers "construct" the meaning. In the restaurant example, the reader is able to infer that Mary sat at a table, selected her meal from the menu, and was probably served by the attendant. Yet none of this information is expressly mentioned in the text. These

The meaning constructed from the same text can vary greatly among people because of differences in the knowledge they possess.

9

details are constructed from the reader's other knowledge of restaurants.

The meaning constructed from the same text can vary greatly among people because of differences in the knowledge they possess.[5] Sometimes people do not have enough knowledge to understand a text, or they may have knowledge that they do not use fully. Variations in interpretation often arise because people have different conceptions about the topic than the author supposed.

Some children may completely lack knowledge on a particular topic, others may know something, while still others may know a lot. Research shows that such differences in knowledge influence children's understanding. For example, in one study, second-grade children equivalent in overall reading ability were given a test of knowledge about spiders prior to reading a selection about spiders.[6] Then they were asked questions about the selection. Children who were more familiar with spiders were significantly better at answering the questions, particularly questions that required reasoning.

Research reveals that children are not good at drawing on their prior knowledge, especially in school settings.[7] They may know something relevant, but yet not use it when trying to understand a passage. These failures are more likely to happen when understanding the passage requires children to extend their knowledge to a somewhat different situation. Even a subtle difference between a child's interpretation and the "right" adult interpretation can give rise to the impression that the child doesn't understand the material.

The second principle is that *reading must be fluent.* The foundation of fluency is the ability to identify individual words. Since English is an alphabetic language, there is a fairly regular connection between the spelling of a word and its pronunciation. Every would-be reader must "break the code" that relates spelling to sound and meaning. Research suggests that, no matter which strategies are used to introduce them to reading, the children who earn the best scores on reading comprehension tests in the second grade are the ones who

Even a subtle difference between a child's interpretation and the "right" adult interpretation can give rise to the impression that the child doesn't understand the material.

made the most progress in fast and accurate word identification in the first grade.[8]

"Decoding" a word — that is, identifying its pronunciation and meaning — involves more than letter by letter analysis. It has been known since late in the 19th century that short, familiar words can be read as fast as single letters and that, under some conditions, words can be identified when the separate letters cannot be.[9] These facts would be impossible if the first step in word identification were always identification of the constituent letters and their sounds. More recently, it has been shown that a meaningful context speeds word identification.[10] For instance, *nurse* is more readily identified if it is preceded by *doctor*. Again, this is a fact that is impossible to square with the common theory that word identification consists of letter by letter decoding.

All of the known facts are understandable within the generally-accepted current model of word identification.[11] According to this model, a possible interpretation of a word usually begins forming in the mind as soon as even partial information has been gleaned about the letters in the word. The possible interpretation reinforces the analysis of the remaining information contained in the letters. When enough evidence from the letters and the context becomes available, the possible interpretation becomes a positive identification. This all happens very quickly, within 250 milliseconds on the average, when the reader is skilled.[12]

Readers must be able to decode words quickly and accurately so that this process can coordinate fluidly with the process of constructing the meaning of the text. One piece of evidence that this is so is that good readers are consistently much faster than poor readers at pronouncing pseudowords that have regular English spellings, such as *tob* and *jate*.[13] People with more than fourth-grade reading ability make almost no mistakes with regular pseudowords. What distinguishes good and poor readers in this case is speed, not accuracy. What this fact means is that typically poor readers have barely mastered spelling-to-sound patterns, whereas good read-

> Readers must be able to decode words quickly and accurately so that this process can coordinate fluidly with the process of constructing the meaning of the text.

ers have a command that goes beyond simple mastery to automaticity.

Interestingly, it does not appear that skilled readers identify unfamiliar words by rapidly applying "rules" governing the relationships between letters and sounds. Instead, research suggests that they work by analogy with known words.[14] Thus, for example, the pronunciation of *tob* may be worked out from knowledge of the pronunication of *job* plus a notion of the initial sound of words beginning with *t*. One piece of evidence in support of the decoding-by-analogy strategy is the fact that pseudowords such as *mave*, which have conflicting possible analogies, such as *have* and *wave*, are pronounced more slowly than other pseudowords, and are sometimes pronounced with a short *a* like *have* and are sometimes pronounced with a long *a* like *wave*. Notice that for the process to work the reader need not have any specific knowledge of the difference between long and short *a*'s, only an adequate vocabulary of actual words and a command of the analogy strategy.

Decoding skill must develop to the point where it is automatic and requires little conscious attention. The reader's attention must be available to interpret the text, rather than to figure out the words. Immature readers are sometimes unable to focus on meaning during reading because they have such a low level of decoding skill. They are directing most of their attention to sounding out words letter by letter or syllable by syllable.[15] Even skilled readers show much less understanding of what they read when forced to attend to the surface features of written material.[16]

Consider, for example, the way a young child might read the first sentence of the restaurant passage:

> When Mary arrived at the r, ruh, ruh, ruh-es-tah,
> oh! restaurant! When Mary arrived at the ... rest...
> restaurant...

Restaurant is a difficult word for this child, and he or she requires several attempts to decode it. By this time, the child's memory for the earlier part of the phrase has faded and he or she has to reread the words to try and create a coherent meaning.

Available figures suggest that an average third grader can read an unfamiliar story aloud at the rate of about 100 words per minute.[17] The corresponding rate for poor readers at this level is 50 to 70 words per minute. According to one group of scholars, this rate is "so slow as to interfere with comprehension even of easy material, and is certainly unlikely to leave much ... capacity free for developing new comprehension abilities."[18]

The third principle is that *reading must be strategic.* Skilled readers are flexible. How they read depends upon the complexity of the text, their familiarity with the topic, and their purpose for reading. Studies show that immature readers lack two strategies used by skilled readers: Assessing their own knowledge relative to the demands of the task, and monitoring their comprehension and implementing fix-up strategies when comprehension fails.[19]

Skilled readers are aware that there are different purposes for reading and that they must change the way they read in response to these purposes. For instance, they know that reading for enjoyment does not require detailed understanding, while reading for a test may. In one study, third and sixth graders were asked to read two stories, one for fun and the other in preparation for a test.[20] The skilled readers adjusted their reading strategies for the two stories; the immature readers didn't. As a result, the immature readers did not remember any more of the story they were supposed to study than the one they were supposed to read for fun.

Perhaps because they frequently do not see the point of reading, poor readers often do not adequately control the way they read. One aspect of such control is being able to monitor one's own reading and notice when failures occur. To investigate this, researchers have placed inconsistent information in passages to see whether readers can detect it. Here are examples of consistent and inconsistent passages:

> All the people who work on this ship get along very well. The people who make a lot of money and the people who don't make much are still friends. The

Skilled readers are flexible. How they read depends upon the complexity of the text, their familiarity with the topic, and their purpose for reading.

13

officers treat me as an equal. We often eat our meals together. I guess we are just one big happy family.

All the people who work on this ship get along very well. The people who make a lot of money and the people who don't make much are still friends. The officers treat me like dirt. We often eat our meals together. I guess we are just one big happy family.[21]

Skilled readers readily detect the inconsistency in the second passage. Younger or less able readers are not as likely to notice the problem and usually say that the passage makes sense.[22]

Another aspect of control during reading is being able to take corrective action once a failure in understanding has been detected. Skilled readers know what to do if they have difficulty. There are a number of options available: Keeping the problem "on hold" in the hope that it will be clarified later in the text; rereading parts of the text; looking ahead; or seeking help from outside sources. In one study, researchers asked second and sixth graders questions about their strategies for coping with failures to understand.[23] Older and better readers said that, for instance, if they did not know the meaning of a word they would ask someone else or go to a dictionary. Poorer readers were unable to say what they would do. These reports have been confirmed by actually observing children. In another study, fourth graders were asked to read and remember a story containing some difficult words.[24] They were given paper, a pencil, and a dictionary and told that they could ask questions. As expected, the good readers asked questions, took notes, and used the dictionary. The poor readers used these aids infrequently.

Throughout this report, the idea that skilled reading needs to be strategic will be emphasized. This means that the reader monitors progress in understanding, and resolves problems that prevent understanding.

The fourth principle is that *reading requires motivation.* As every teacher knows, motivation is one of the keys to learning to read. It will take most children several years to learn to read well. Somehow, their attention must be sustained during this period and they must not lose the hope that eventually they will become successful readers.

Reading itself is fun. At least, it is for many children who are skilled readers for their age and for some children with average and below average skill. These children are, as the saying goes, "hooked on books." Increasing the proportion of children who read widely and with evident satisfaction ought to be as much a goal of reading instruction as increasing the number who are competent readers. As will be detailed in the chapter on Extending Literacy, an essential step in reaching that goal is providing children ready access to books that are interesting to them.

Reading instruction can be boring. Aspects of the standard reading lesson are monotonous. Many of the tasks assigned to children in the name of reading are drudgery. Thus, it is not surprising that in one study, for instance, interviews with a sample of poor, black children reading a year above grade level indicated that most liked to read, but few liked the activities called "reading" in school.[25]

Teachers who maintain high levels of motivation conduct fast-paced and varied lessons. Tasks are introduced with enthusiasm and with explanations of why doing them will help one become a better reader. Teachers whose classes are motivated are described as business-like but supportive and friendly. Children taught by teachers rated as having these traits make larger-than-average gains on reading achievement tests.[26]

Failure is not fun. Predictably, poor readers have unfavorable attitudes toward reading. What is not so predictable is whether lack of proficiency in reading stems from unfavorable attitudes or whether it is the other way around. Probably the truth can lie in either direction.

Poor readers frequently are listless and inattentive and sometimes are disruptive. They do not complete work. They give up quickly when faced with a task that is difficult for them. They become anxious when they must read aloud or take a test. A good summary

> Teachers whose classes are motivated are described as business-like but supportive and friendly.

15

description is that they act as though they were helpless to do better.[27]

The etiology of this sense of helplessness is not completely understood, but it is known that it is affected in sometimes subtle ways by teachers' behavior. It might be thought an act of kindness to express pity when students flub a test, but the hidden message may be that they lack the ability to do any better, that they are not in control of their own fate. An expression of dissatisfaction, on the other hand, may convey the message that the students could do better if they tried harder. People can control effort; people in control, even ones doing poorly, are not helpless.[28]

Effective reading teachers convey by word and deed that everyone can learn to read, if they pay attention and apply themselves. In their classrooms, effort pays off. Research establishes that these teachers assign reading material on which children experience a high rate of success.[29] However, effective teachers do not offer praise indiscriminately. Praise is given in recognition of noteworthy success at a task that is difficult for *this* student. The statement of praise specifies what the student did well, attributes the success to ability and effort, and implies that similar successes are attainable in the future.[30]

Though sustained motivation is essential for learning to read, it should be cautioned that poor motivation is not the only problem, or even the most important problem, faced by poor readers. Experience indicates that even under the best of conditions some percentage of children will have difficulties in learning to read. A detailed discussion of what may be the root causes of these difficulties is beyond the scope of this report. It can be asserted with some confidence, nonetheless, that the approaches to reading outlined in this report can help to ameliorate the difficulties faced by very poor readers. (See Afterword.)

The fifth principle is that *reading is a continuously developing skill.* Reading, like playing a musical instrument, is not something that is mastered once and for all at a certain age. Rather, it is a skill that continues to

Reading, like playing a musical instrument, is not something that is mastered once and for all at a certain age. Rather, it is a skill that continues to improve through practice.

improve through practice. The process begins with a person's earliest exposure to text and a literate culture and continues throughout life.[31]

A good rule of thumb is that the most useful form of practice is doing the whole skill of reading — that is, reading meaningful text for the purpose of understanding the message it contains. This fact poses a problem for the beginner. How can a child practice reading without already being able to read?

One or more of several strategies are used to get a beginner started reading. A natural strategy is to use familiar stories that are readily understandable to the child, or maybe even partly known by heart. A common strategy is to severely restrict the vocabulary of the first selections a beginner will read. Another useful strategy is to teach the beginner something about the relationships between letters and sounds.

Like instruction in other complex skills, reading instruction most often takes the form of explanation, advice, coaching, and practice on what are judged to be the essential aspects or parts of the process. The test of the value of this instruction is whether the child's reading as a whole improves. Thus, in a well-designed reading program, mastering the parts does not become an end in itself, but a means to an end, and there is a proper balance between practice of the parts and practice of the whole.

> In a well-designed reading program, mastering the parts does not become an end in itself, but a means to an end, and there is a proper balance between practice of the parts and practice of the whole.

In summary:

- **Skilled reading is constructive.** Becoming a skilled reader requires learning to reason about written material using knowledge from everyday life and from disciplined fields of study.

- **Skilled reading is fluent.** Becoming a skilled reader depends upon mastering basic processes to the point where they are automatic, so that attention is freed for the analysis of meaning.

- **Skilled reading is strategic.** Becoming a skilled reader requires learning to control one's reading in relation to one's purpose, the nature of the material, and whether one is comprehending.

17

- **Skilled reading is motivated.** Becoming a skilled reader requires learning to sustain attention and learning that written material can be interesting and informative.

- **Skilled reading is a lifelong pursuit.** Becoming a skilled reader is a matter of continuous practice, development, and refinement.

Reading must be seen as part of a child's general language development and not as a discrete skill isolated from listening, speaking, and writing.

Emerging Literacy

This chapter details the critical first steps in learning to read. The first major section describes the role played by experience with reading and language in the home. The second major section deals with reading instruction in the kindergarten. The third major section deals with systematic reading instruction. Systematic reading instruction begins no later than the first grade, and, today, may begin in kindergarten.

Reading and the Home

Reading begins in the home. To a greater or lesser degree, depending upon the home, children acquire knowledge before coming to school that lays the foundation for reading.[1] They acquire concepts for understanding things, events, thoughts, and feelings, and the oral language vocabulary for expressing these concepts. They acquire the basic grammar of oral language.

To a greater or lesser degree, children acquire specific knowledge about written language before coming to school. Some children even learn to read at home. Almost all children learn something about the forms of stories, how to ask and answer questions, and how to recognize a few, or sometimes many, letters and words.

Early development of the knowledge required for

Early development of the knowledge required for reading comes from experience talking and learning about the world and talking and learning about written language.

21

reading comes from experience talking and learning about the world and talking and learning about written language. Once children are in school, parents' expectations and home language and experience continue to influence how much and how well children read.

Talking and Learning About the World

Reading depends upon wide knowledge.[2] The more knowledge children are able to acquire at home, the greater their chance for success in reading. For example, many textbooks have selections about history and nature. Even understanding simple stories can depend on having common and not so common knowledge. Children who have gone on trips, walked in parks, and gone to zoos and museums will have more background knowledge relevant to school reading than children who have not had these experiences.

Wide experience alone is not enough, however. The way in which parents *talk* to their children about an experience influences what knowledge the children will gain from the experience and their later ability to draw on the knowledge when reading. It is talk about experience that extends the child's stock of concepts and associated vocabulary.[3]

The content of statements and questions and the manner in which they are phrased influence what children will learn from experience. Questions can be phrased in ways that require children merely to put some part of an experience into words or they can be phrased in a thought-provoking manner. For example, one parent may ask a child, "What do you see under the windshield wiper?", while another may ask, "Why do you think there's a slip of paper under the windshield wiper?" Thought-provoking questions stimulate the intellectual growth needed for success in reading.

Research suggests that it is important for parents to encourage children to think about events removed from the immediate here and now.[4] In some homes, conversations center around ongoing events. For example, the topic of conversation may be the clothes the child is putting on or the food that is being eaten for dinner.

The way in which parents *talk* to their children about experience influences what knowledge the children will gain from the experience and their later ability to draw on the knowledge when reading.

In other homes, parents often ask children to describe events in which the parents did not participate, such as a nursery school outing or a visit to a friend's home. This appears to require children to exercise their memories, to reflect on experience, and to learn to give complete descriptions and tell complete stories.

Children who have extended conversations at home that make them reflect upon experience learn to contruct meaning from events. They have a subsequent advantage in learning to read. A long-term study that followed children from age one to seven found that the content and style of the language parents used with their children predicted the children's school achievement in reading.[5]

Talking and Learning About Written Language

While a rich background of experience and the oral language facility to discuss this experience provide an essential foundation, the specific abilities required for reading come from immediate experience with written language. The principle that children learn to read by being taught to read is as true at home as it is in school. The most effective mode for instruction in the home, however, may take a different form than it does at school.

The single most important activity for building the knowledge required for eventual success in reading is reading aloud to children.[6] This is especially so during the preschool years. The benefits are greatest when the child is an active participant, engaging in discussions about stories, learning to identify letters and words, and talking about the meanings of words. One researcher who observed parents reading books to their children discovered differences in the quality and quantity of informal instruction that the parents provided.[7] Some parents asked questions similar to those that teachers ask in school. Thus, their children had experience playing school-like question and answer games. These parents also related the episodes in books to real life events. For example, if parent and child saw a rabbit, the parent might compare the event with one in a book such as *Peter Rabbit*.

The single most important activity for building the knowledge required for eventual success in reading is reading aloud to children.

23

Other parents asked children perfunctory questions about stories being read or did not discuss what was being read. Not surprisingly, children whose parents asked few questions or only questions that required repetition of facts from stories achieved less well in school reading than children whose parents asked questions that required thinking and who related story happenings to real life events.[8]

Stories aren't the only material that provide children with exposure to written language. Records or tapes with follow-along books recently have been marketed to help young children learn to read. There is some support for the use of records or tapes in classroom reading activities,[9] and the use of such materials in the home may also be beneficial.

Such old-fashioned materials as chalkboards and paper and pencils can make a difference in children's learning to read. When children who learned to read before going to school were compared to similar children who couldn't read, the early readers were found to have greater access to chalkboards and paper and pencils and to do more writing.[10] Writing gives children a way to practice letter-sound relationships. Magnetic boards and letters can be used with young children who can't yet write with a pencil and may also promote the development of letter-sound knowledge.[11]

Many parents tutor preschool children in elements of reading, such as letter names.[12] Parents can do this through formal means such as workbooks or through opportunities that arise informally as part of everyday activities. Examples of informal instruction are pointing out letters on signs or writing messages on a magnetic board. In the home, informal instruction seems to work as well or better than formal, systematic approaches. Evidence of this comes from a study in which one group of parents was trained to teach their children to name letters and to identify sounds using a workbook. Children in another group, whose parents simply read to them, performed as well on beginning reading tasks as those whose parents had the training and the workbooks.[13]

For informal teaching to be successful, parents must be aware of what their children can learn and the experiences through which such learning will occur. They must know the importance of such matters as pointing out letters from the child's name on signs and containers. In a study comparing kindergarten children's knowledge, those who knew a lot about written language had parents who believed that it was their responsibility to seize opportunities to convey information about written language to their children.[14] Parents of children who had little knowledge did not share this belief.

Parents can affect children's learning from television programs that teach preschoolers about reading.[15] For example, parents can make sure that their children see the program regularly, and ask their children questions about the show to help them learn from it. Also important are parents' efforts to relate the program to other situations. For example, if children have learned the letter *m* and the sound associated with it on the show, drawing attention to other examples of words beginning with *m* is useful.

Computer software companies are developing beginning reading programs aimed at the lucrative home market. At this time, there is little solid information about the impact of computers on children's reading. However, a computer is an extraordinarily versatile piece of equipment, and it is only reasonable to suppose that it could play a useful role in learning to read.

The quality of the instruction incorporated in the computer software is sure to be paramount. Some software packages probably will provide children with good experiences; others probably will be nothing more than automated worksheets. Parents need to shop carefully for software packages that provide worthwhile reading experiences. Furthermore, simply placing children in front of a computer terminal with a reading software program probably won't teach them to read. Based on accumulated experience with other media, it seems likely that even satisfactory reading software will have greater benefits if parents are actively involved in the ways suggested throughout this section.

Children who knew a lot about written language had parents who believed that it was their responsibility to seize oportunities to convey information about written language to their children.

25

Talking and Learning About Reading at School

Throughout the school years, parents continue to influence children's reading through monitoring of school performance, support for homework, and, most important, continued personal involvement with their children's growth as readers. Research shows that parents of successful readers have a more accurate view of their children's performance.[16] These parents know about the school's reading program. They visit their children's teachers, may observe in classrooms periodically, and are more likely to participate in home-school liaison programs.

In a study of children's achievement in the United States, Taiwan, and Japan, American parents were found to consider homework to be of less value than Japanese or Taiwanese parents.[17] Perhaps as a consequence, American children spend much less time on homework than the Japanese or Taiwanese children. Studies in the United States show a small to moderate relationship between the amount of time students spend doing homework and their reading achievement.[18]

Depending upon the kind of homework they assign, teachers have been found to foster or undermine parental support. Some teachers ask students to complete worksheets at home, rather than asking them to read books, magazines, or newspapers (see below).[19] Many of these worksheets are of questionable value in the classroom; they are even more so in the home. Parents sometimes perceive assignments as busywork. This irritates them. Parents may be asked to help with tasks that they cannot do themselves. This antagonizes them.

Most children will learn *how* to read. Whether they *will* read depends in part upon encouragement from their parents. Several researchers recently studied the amount of reading that middle-grade students do at home.[20] Those who read a lot show larger gains on reading achievement tests. They tend to come from homes in which there are plenty of books, or opportunities to visit the library, and in which parents and brothers and sisters also read. Their parents suggest reading as a leisure time activity and make sure there is time for reading. For example, some limit TV watching or have an established bedtime hour after which reading is the only activity permitted other than going to sleep.

Parents of avid readers favor having teachers require students to read library books and believe that their children read more when teachers do so.[21] However, they do not endorse required reading of particular books. They favor the principle of allowing their children to choose their own books, although they acknowledge that they themselves disapprove of an occasional choice.

Parents often ask about the effect of television on reading. Within reason, television viewing does not appear to interfere with learning to read. Up to about ten hours a week, there is actually a slight positive relationship between the amount of time children spend watching TV and their school achievement, including reading achievement.[22] Beyond this point, the relationship turns negative and, as the number of hours of viewing per week climbs, achievement declines sharply.

There is evidence that confirms that TV programs especially designed to have educational value for young children do in fact promote reading.[23] Further, a dramatization of a novel or an animated production of a favorite cartoon strip can encourage children to read the book or the newspaper. Though research does not prove the point, common sense suggests that, depending on the age of the child, documentaries, newscasts, good drama, and wildlife, natural history, and science shows will also contribute to reading achievement. On the other hand, programs that are unlikely to have any redeeming educational value will come readily to any parent's mind. Prudent parents will want to influence the quality of the programs their children watch as well as maintain reasonable limits on the amount of viewing.

In conclusion, parents play roles of inestimable importance in laying the foundation for learning to read. A parent is a child's first guide through a vast and unfamiliar world. A parent is a child's first mentor on what words mean and how to mean things with words.

Parents play roles of inestimable importance in laying the foundation for learning to read. A parent is a child's first tutor in unraveling the fascinating puzzle of written language. A parent is a child's one enduring source of faith that somehow, sooner or later, he or she will become a good reader.

27

A parent is a child's first tutor in unraveling the fascinating puzzle of written language. A parent is a child's one enduring source of faith that somehow, sooner or later, he or she will become a good reader.

On a more sober note, parents' good intentions for their children are not enough. Parents must put their intentions into practice if their children are to have the foundation required for success in reading.

Reading Instruction in Kindergarten

Until the 1960s, kindergartens served primarily as a transition between home and school. Children learned to work with unfamiliar adults, get along with other children, and adjust to the routine of school. Traditional kindergartens also aimed to convey a variety of kinds of common knowledge and to develop general social, physical, and intellectual skills. Kindergartens still serve these functions, but now, in addition, there is an increasing expectation that systematic reading instruction will begin in kindergarten. Indeed, in many communities today kindergartens employ a simplified version of what used to be first-grade reading instruction.

The changing expectations for kindergarten stem from a new understanding of what children are capable of learning, which will be detailed in the next section, and also from recent trends in the society, notably the steady increase in the number of working women with young children. These children attend nursery schools and daycare centers that socialize them to school and develop some of the knowledge and skill formerly acquired in kindergarten.

When Should Systematic Reading Instruction Begin?

According to a view dating back to the 1930's, children are "ready" to learn to read only when they reach a certain level of maturity.[24] The typical child was thought to reach this level at the age of about six and one-half, though the time might be earlier or later for particular children depending upon their physical, social, and intellectual development. Until a child reached the requisite level of maturity, it was believed that systematic reading instruction would be unproductive or even harmful.

There is a kernel of good sense in the idea of readiness for instruction. Formal, organized instruction may be unproductive for children who still cry when their mothers leave them at school, who cannot sit still in their seats, or who cannot follow simple directions. However, the concept of readiness, as it was formulated in the decades following 1930, has proved to be too global.

In the past, under the belief that it would develop readiness for reading, kindergarten children were taught to hop and skip, cut with a scissors, name the colors, and tell the difference between circles and squares. These may be worthwhile activities for four- and five-year-olds, but skill in doing them has a negligible relationship with learning to read.[25] There are schools, nonetheless, that still use reading readiness checklists that assess kicking a ball, skipping, or hopping. Thus, reading instruction is delayed for some children because they have failed to master these physical skills or other skills with a doubtful relationship to reading.

What the child who is least ready for systematic reading instruction needs most is ample experience with oral and printed language, and early opportunities to begin to write. These are the topics of the next three sections.

When should systematic reading instruction begin, then? There is a wealth of evidence that children can benefit from early reading and language instruction in preschool and kindergarten.[26] Available data suggest that the best short-term results are obtained from programs that can be characterized as formal, structured, and intensive,[27] though whether these programs have greater long-term benefits is less clear. Good results are also obtained with informal, though not haphazard, programs.[28]

Based on the best evidence available at the present time, the Commission favors a balanced kindergarten program in reading and language that includes both formal and informal approaches. The important point

What the child who is least ready for systematic reading instruction needs most is ample experience with oral and printed language, and early opportunities to begin to write.

29

is that instruction should be systematic but free from undue pressure. We advise caution in being so impatient for our children that we turn kindergartens, and even nursery schools and daycare centers, into academic bootcamps.

Developing Oral Language

Reading must be seen as part of a child's general language development and not as a discrete skill isolated from listening, speaking, and writing. Reading instruction builds especially on oral language. If this foundation is weak, progress in reading will be slow and uncertain. Children must have at least a basic vocabulary, a reasonable range of knowledge about the world around them, and the ability to talk about their knowledge. These abilities form the basis for comprehending text.

Listening comprehension proficiency in kindergarten and first grade is a moderately good predictor of the level of reading comprehension attained by the third grade.[29] Evidence about the later role of listening comprehension is even stronger. In a study involving a nationwide sample of thousands of students, listening comprehension in the fifth grade was the best predictor of performance on a range of aptitude and achievement tests in high school, better than any other measure of aptitude or achievement in the fifth grade.[30]

Oral language experience in the classroom is especially important for children who have not grown up with oral language that resembles the language of schools and books. As the discussion of home experiences in the previous section revealed, some children have not been required to use language in reflective ways at home. When adult questions require children to reflect upon their experiences, mental processes that are needed for proficient reading are stimulated. Thus, kindergarten teachers need to capitalize on every opportunity to engage children in thoughtful discussion. Storybook reading is an especially good setting for such discussions. As they listen to stories, and discuss them, children will learn to make inferences about plots and characters.

While oral language facility is necessary for success

in reading, it is not sufficient. To learn to read, children's environment must also be rich in experiences with written language.

Learning About Written Language

Children enter a typical kindergarten class with very different levels of knowledge about printed language,[31] and instruction needs to be adapted for these differences. One or two children, and sometimes more, may already be able to read simple stories. A handful may be totally unfamiliar with such basic concepts as a word, a sentence, and a letter, and may not even know that to read you hold a book right side up and turn the pages from front to back. Most children entering kindergarten today, however, will know more about reading and writing than children did a decade or two ago.

A staple of kindergarten reading instruction is teaching children to name the letters of the alphabet. However, increasing numbers of children can already do this when they enter kindergarten. In a 1984 study, beginning kindergarten children from a variety of backgrounds could name an average of 14 letters.[32]

Children's proficiency in letter naming when they start school is an excellent predictor of their first- and second-grade reading achievement.[33] This fact seemingly supports the practice of having kindergartners learn letter names. Probably, however, knowledge of letter names is not important in itself so much as it is a reflection of broader knowledge about reading and language. This conclusion follows from the further fact that, when children who do not know the letter names on entering kindergarten are trained to name them, they show little later advantage in reading. In contrast, children taught the sounds letters make, as well as their names, show better reading achievement than children who receive only instruction in letter names.[34]

Research establishes that children learning to read require concepts about the broader purposes of printed language, as well as the specific skills required to recognize letters and words and match letters and sounds.[35] Learning about reading and writing ought to occur in

Children enter a typical kindergarten class with very different levels of knowledge about printed language, and instruction needs to be adapted for these differences.

31

situations where written language serves functions such as to entertain (as in books), to inform (as in instructions on packages), or to direct (as on traffic signs). In other words, children need to learn about the functions of written language and about what adults mean when they talk about "reading". Children must also learn about the relationship between oral and written language and the relationship between written language and meaning. For example, they need to know about the relationship between the letter combination STOP, the spoken word "stop", and the meaning of *stop* — to cease motion.

Even children from homes where adults have not provided them with extensive exposure to printed language have some knowledge about reading and writing that can form the basis for early instruction. For instance, they may be able to recognize words that appear on cereal boxes, t-shirts, billboards, or toys. However, they often jump to incorrect conclusions about words: They may think that the brand name on a toothpaste tube says "toothpaste" or "brush your teeth," indicating that they are paying more attention to the context than to the specific features of the word. Nonetheless, familiar words are especially useful for teaching children letter names and letter-sound relationships, because children can learn to recognize familiar words prior to knowing all the letters.[36]

Young children enjoy hearing the same story read over and over again, a fact that can be used as a fulcrum for beginning reading instruction. Books such as *This is the House That Jack Built* contain repeated phrases that make it possible for children to participate by reading the repetitive part with an adult. Through reading along, children achieve what one writer calls "wholebooksuccess": They get the satisfaction of reading real books.[37] After a story has been read in this fashion, words from the story can be printed on charts and sentence strips so that the children can begin to recognize the words outside the helpful context of the familiar book.

In conclusion, kindergarten teachers must be mindful of the fact that there can be an extraordinarily wide variation in the knowledge that kindergarteners have about reading. Some children may not have even the most basic ideas. When a concept such as a word and concepts about the functions of printed language are taken for granted by teachers and the publishers of instructional materials, children can be left huffing and puffing over the sounds that letters make with only the faintest idea of what they are doing. Early instruction must provide these children with underlying concepts about the functions of reading and writing as well as with specific information about letters, sounds, and words. On the other hand, for those who come to kindergarten already reading simple stories, none of this basic teaching may be necessary. Thus, the essential principle of all good teaching — estimate where each student is and build on that base — is doubly important for kindergarten teachers.

Learning to Write

Writing is important in its own right. Because of the interrelatedness of language, learning to write also aids in reading development. For many young children, the desire to communicate provides an incentive for using written language. In an investigation of children who read before they entered first grade, the parents described these children as "paper-and-pencil kids".[38] For some, in fact, learning to read was a byproduct of interest in writing.

Writing experience in the kindergarten should not overemphasize handwriting practice. In addition to beginning to learn to print, children need to learn that writing is composing a message using their own words to communicate with other people. Children can do quite a bit of writing before they are able to use a pencil well. For example, preformed plastic and metal letters used on felt or magnetic boards allow young children to write without the constraints of handwriting. In the early 1960's, a program in which preschoolers wrote on typewriters reported success in teaching children to read.[39] Currently, data are being gathered on the value for preschool children of simple word processing programs on microcomputers. As their motor coordination improves, children will acquire greater facility with pencils and pens. Until that point, however, they can have much-needed experience with writing using means that do not require them to form letters by hand.

When children do not feel too constrained by requirements for correct spelling and penmanship, writing activities provide a good opportunity for them to apply and extend their knowledge of letter-sound correspondences.[40] Many preschool children's spelling does not comply with standard spellings. In time, these children will use standard spellings but not before moving through the fairly well-documented stage of "invented" spelling.[41] For example, children may initially write *t* for the word *tame*. Several months later, this may become *tm*, followed by *tam*, and finally *tame*.

Children's spelling becomes more conventional and they become facile at handwriting if they are given numerous opportunities for writing.[42] Reasons for writing can be found in any kindergarten classroom. For example, children can write captions for their pictures or address invitations. Their initial attempts may be only a single letter or word. Next they may move on to a phrase, such as "I love you," as they write a note to a favorite adult. These writing activities lay the foundation for letter writing and story writing. They also provide children with reasons to communicate, to apply their knowledge of written language, and to read their own writing and that of others.

Reading in the First Grade

Today many children begin to receive formal reading instruction in kindergarten. Once they reach the first grade, no matter what their kindergarten reading experience has been, it is virtually certain that they will receive formal, or structured, instruction. In most classrooms, the instruction will be driven by a basal reading program. For this reason, the importance of these programs cannot be underestimated and will be briefly discussed here.

> When children do not feel too constrained by requirements for correct spelling and penmanship, writing activities provide a good opportunity for them to apply and extend their knowledge of letter-sound correspondences.

Basal Reading Programs

Basal reading programs are complete packages of teaching materials. They provide an entire reading curriculum (summarized in what is called a "scope and sequence chart"), instructional strategies for teaching reading (through teachers' manuals), a graded anthology of selections for children to read (through student Readers), and practice exercises (through workbooks and skill sheets). In addition, there are numerous optional and supplementary materials (e.g., management and testing systems; visual aids such as word cards, sentence cards and picture cards; audio tapes; film strips; supplementary books). Basal reading programs are organized by grade level with most programs beginning at kindergarten and continuing through the eighth grade. An entire basal reading program would make a stack of books and papers four feet high.

The observation that basal programs "drive" reading instruction is not to be taken lightly. These programs strongly influence how reading is taught in American schools and what students read. This influence is demonstrated by studies that have examined how time and instructional materials are used in classrooms. The estimates are that basal reading programs account for from 75 percent to 90 percent of what goes on during reading periods in elementary school classrooms.[43]

How closely do teachers follow basal reading programs? A number of classroom studies indicate that, for the most part, teachers follow the instructional strategies prescribed in the teachers' manuals and that students use the Readers and workbook materials.[44] These studies do not suggest, however, that teachers use *all* of the available materials, or that they incorporate all of the recommended procedures in the teachers' manuals. Yet, the studies conclude that basal programs account for a large part of teachers' and students' time during the reading period.

Basal reading programs typically are developed by teams of authors who work with editors of educational publishing companies. These companies market their programs to schools throughout the United States. Al-

The observation that basal programs "drive" reading instruction is not to be taken lightly. These programs strongly influence how reading is taught in American schools and what students read.

though over a dozen well-known basal reading programs are on the market, about 70 percent of American schools buy one or more of the five best-selling programs. While membership in the "top five" varies from decade to decade, it can be asserted with a fair degree of certainty that a small number of basal reading programs have a strong influence on *how* American children are taught to read and *what* American children read.

Word Recognition and Beginning Reading

One of the cornerstones of skilled reading is fast, accurate word identification.[45] Well into the 20th century almost all children in this country were started on the road to skilled word identification by teaching them the letters of the alphabet, the sounds the letters make, and, using this knowledge, how to sound out words. During the first third of this century, educators such as William S. Gray were responsible for turning American schools away from what they perceived to be the "heartless drudgery" of the traditional approach.[46] In its place, Gray and others advocated the look-and-say approach. The thinking was that children would make more rapid progress in reading if they identified whole words at a glance, as adults seem to do.

The look-say approach gradually came to dominate the teaching of beginning reading.[47] Nonetheless, educators continued to debate the best way to introduce children to reading. Rudolph Flesch brought the debate forcibly to the public's attention in the mid-1950s with his book, *Why Johnny Can't Read,* in which he mounted a scathing attack against the look-say method and advocated a return to phonics.[48] More influential in professional circles, though, was Jeanne Chall's now-classic book a decade later, *Learning to Read: The Great Debate.* Chall concluded on the basis of evidence available at the time that programs that included phonics as one component were superior to those that did not.[49]

The question, then, is how should children be taught to read words? The answer given by most reading educators today is that phonics instruction is one of the essential ingredients. All the major published reading

The issue is no longer, as it was several decades ago, whether children should be taught phonics. The issues now are specific ones of just how it should be done.

programs include material for teaching phonics to beginning readers. Thus, the issue is no longer, as it was several decades ago, whether children should be taught phonics. The issues now are specific ones of just how it should be done.

Intuitively it makes sense that beginning readers receive phonics instruction because English is an alphabetic language in which there are consistent, though not entirely predictable, relationships between letters and sounds. When children learn these relationships well, most of the words in their spoken language become accessible to them when they see them in print. When this happens, children are said to have "broken the code."

What does research indicate about the effectiveness of phonics instruction? Classroom research shows that, on the average, children who are taught phonics get off to a better start in learning to read than children who are not taught phonics.[50] The advantage is most apparent on tests of word identification, though children in programs in which phonics gets a heavy stress also do better on tests of sentence and story comprehension, particularly in the early grades.

Data on the long-term effects of phonics instruction are scanty. In one of the few longitudinal studies, children who had received intensive phonics instruction in kindergarten or first grade performed better in the third grade than a comparison group of children on both a word identification test and a comprehension test. By the sixth grade, the group that years earlier had received intensive phonics instruction still did better than the comparison group on a word identification test but the advantage in comprehension had vanished.[51] The fact that an early phonics emphasis had less influence on comprehension as the years passed is probably attributable to the increasing importance of knowledge of the topic, vocabulary, and reasoning ability on advanced comprehension tests.

The picture that emerges from the research is that phonics facilitates word identification and that fast, accurate word identification is a necessary but not suf-

The goal of phonics is not that children be able to state the "rules" governing letter-sound relationships. Rather, the purpose is to get across the alphabetic principle, the principle that there *are* systematic relationships between letters and sounds.

ficient condition for comprehension. More will be said about the need for comprehension instruction in tandem with phonics instruction later. Here, the features that distinguish types of phonics instruction will be discussed.

Issues in the Teaching of Phonics

Phonics is instruction in the relationship between letters and speech sounds. The goal of phonics is not that children be able to state the "rules" governing letter-sound relationships. Rather, the purpose is to get across the alphabetic principle, the principle that there *are* systematic relationships between letters and sounds. Phonics ought to be conceived as a technique for getting children off to a fast start in mapping the relationships between letters and sounds.

It follows that phonics instruction should aim to teach only the most important and regular of letter-to-sound relationships, because this is the sort of instruction that will most directly lay bare the alphabetic principle. Once the basic relationships have been taught, the best way to get children to refine and extend their knowledge of letter-sound correspondences is through repeated opportunities to read. If this position is correct, then much phonics instruction is overly subtle and probably unproductive. For instance, many reading programs not only teach the speech sounds represented by the letters *b*, *l*, and *r*, but then they go on to directly teach the sounds associated with *bl* as in *black* and *br* as in *break*. This instruction is provided even to children who can read words containing *bl* and *br* flawlessly!

Thus, a number of reading programs, including ones not known for providing intensive phonics, try to teach too many letter-sound relationships and phonics instruction drags out over too many years. These programs seem to be making the dubious assumption that exposure to a vast set of phonics relationships will enable a child to produce perfect pronunciations of words. The more reasonable assumption is that phonics can help the child come up with approximate pronunciations — candidates that have to be checked to see whether they match words known from spoken language that fit in the context of the story being read.

The best way to get children to refine and extend their knowledge of letter-sound correspondences is through repeated opportunities to read.

There are essentially two approaches to phonics instruction — explicit phonics and implicit phonics.[52] The following discussion will address only the major differences between the two approaches. In practice, there are similarities in the instructional strategies used in explicit and implicit phonics programs as well as differences among explicit programs and among implicit programs.

In explicit phonics instruction, the sounds associated with letters are identified in isolation and then "blended" together to form words. For example, the teacher may write the letter *s* on the chalkboard and tell the children that the letter makes the sound /s/, or point to the *s* in the word *sat* and say that it begins with /s/.[53] During a typical explicit phonics lesson, the children will be asked to produce the sounds of letters that appear in isolation and in words.[54]

A critical step in explicit phonics instruction is blending the isolated sounds of letters to produce words. To help children blend the sounds in the word *sit,* for example, a teacher may begin by pointing to each letter and asking the children to say the separate sounds, /s/ /i/ /t/. Next the teacher may model blending by extending the sounds /ssiit/ and then collapsing the sounds together to yield *sit.*

Blending may seem simple to an adult who already knows how to read, but in fact it is a difficult step for many children. Until a child gets over this hurdle, learning the sounds of individual letters and groups of letters will have diminished value. Research indicates that teachers who spend more than average amounts of time on blending produce larger than average gains on first- and second-grade reading achievement tests.[55] Regrettably, an analysis of published reading programs concluded that several incorporate procedures for teaching blending that are unlikely to be effective with many children.[56]

In implicit phonics instruction, the sound associated with a letter is never supposed to be pronounced in isolation. Instead, in an implicit program the teacher might write a list of words on the board such as *sand,*

A number of reading programs, including ones not known for providing intensive phonics, try to teach too many letter-sound relationships and phonics instruction drags out over too many years.

39

soft, slip, and ask the children what all the words have in common. When the letter name *s* has been elicited the teacher would tell the children that, "The letter *s* stands for the sound you hear at the beginning of *sand, soft,* and *slip.*" To figure out the sound of a letter in a word to be read, children receiving implicit phonic instruction may be told, "This word begins with the letter *s,* so you know the word begins with the sound for *s*" or "think about other words you know that begin with the same letter."[57]

How is phonics taught in this country? No large-scale descriptions are available, but the fact that the most widely-used reading programs employ implicit phonic instruction suggests that this is the most prevalent way. However, classroom observation suggests that some teachers, at least, may not always follow the principle of implicit phonics. In a recent study, several first-grade teachers ostensibly using one or another implicit phonic program were observed.[58] Contrary to the recommendations in the teachers' manuals, they all produced the separate sounds of consonants and vowels apart from words. When asked why they did this, the teachers gave similar explanations. In the words of one of them, "That's how they hear it [the speech sound] best."

Analyses have revealed some specific problems with both implicit and explicit phonics. A problem with implicit phonics is that it places stress on an ability called "phonemic segmentation." This is the ability to identify separate speech sounds in spoken words. There is evidence that many young children cannot extract an individual sound from hearing it within a word.[59] This ability may depend upon already having learned something about the sounds associated with the separate letters. For instance, children who do not already have some idea of the sounds of the letters in *sit* may not be able to single out the short /i/ sound when they hear the word spoken. Hence, when the teacher tells the children that the letter *i,* "has the sound you hear in the middle of *sit,*" they may not be able to make the connection. Ironically, therefore, implicit phonics may actually presuppose what it is supposed to teach.

On the other hand, a problem with explicit phonics is that both teachers and children have a difficult time saying pure speech sounds in isolation. The *b* sound becomes /buh/, for instance. When figuring out a new word, the child who has been taught the sounds of letters in isolation may produce /buh-ah-tuh/ and never recognize that the word is *bat*. This problem may be more hypothetical than real, since there does not appear to be evidence that hearing or producing imprecise speech sounds is an actual obstacle to figuring out words, provided that the words are ones the children know from their spoken language and the words are encountered in a meaningful context.

All that phonics can be expected to do is help children get approximate pronunciations. These must be "tried out" to determine whether recognizable words have been produced that make sense in the context. When the process is working smoothly, it is not likely, for instance, that in the course of reading a story about pets a child would read "...dogs and cuh-ah-tuhs."[60]

Some authorities fear that a heavy emphasis on explicit phonics will interfere with the development of skill in meaningful, constructive reading. One basis for this fear comes from the analysis of children's errors during oral reading. Oral reading errors provide a window into what is going on inside children's heads as they read. Research suggests that first graders taught through an explicit phonics approach make more nonsense errors than other children.[61] These are errors that either are not words in English or are English words that make no sense in the story being read.

Other authorities contend that nonsense errors made by beginning readers are merely an indication that children are trying to use information about letters and sounds. Research does suggest that making these errors is a stage that will pass once more fluency is developed and the children have learned to make use of all of the information available about a word's pronunciation and meaning.[62] A recent study found that by the time they had reached the third grade, children who had begun

All that phonics can be expected to do is help children get approximate pronunciations.

41

in the first grade with intensive, explicit phonics were making no more nonsense errors than other children.[63]

Phonics instruction in general has been criticized for leading children away from meaning.[64] Probably, this is not an inherent flaw of either explicit or implicit phonics. It may, however, be a flaw in the design of particular programs. Quite likely the problem is simply a by-product of the false dichotomy between phonics and meaning that has dominated the field of reading for so many years. In an excess of zeal to get phonics across, some programs introduce the sounds of many letters before providing opportunities to use what has been learned in reading words in sentences and stories.

Which works better, then, explicit or implicit phonics? When the criterion is children's year-to-year gains on standardized reading achievement tests, the available research does not permit a decisive answer, although the trend of the data favors explicit phonics.[65]

In the judgment of the Commission, isolating the sounds associated with most letters and teaching children to blend the sounds of letters together to try to identify words are useful instructional strategies. These are the strategies of explicit phonics. However, research provides insufficient justification for strict adherence to either overall philosophy. Probably, the best strategy would draw from both approaches. For example, the sounds of some letters such as *r*, which are especially difficult to produce correctly in isolation, might be introduced best using the implicit approach.

Further, letter-sound relationships should always be lavishly illustrated with words. These provide concrete exemplars for what can otherwise be confusing, abstract rules. When children are encouraged to think of other words they know with similar spellings when they encounter a word they cannot readily identify, they are probably helped to develop the adult strategy of decoding unknown words by analogy with ones that are known.[66] This is a strong feature of the implicit approach, which is intrinsically word based. Of course, explicit phonics programs do illustrate letter-sound relationships with words, but the instruction in some of

The purpose of phonics is to teach children the alphabetic principle. The goal is for this to become an *operating principle* so that young readers consistently use information about the relationship between letters and sounds and letters and meanings to assist in the identification of known words and to independently figure out unfamiliar words.

42

these programs would be strengthened if more attention were paid to systematically providing words to serve as concrete exemplars.

In summary, the purpose of phonics is to teach children the alphabetic principle. The goal is for this to become an *operating principle* so that young readers consistently use information about the relationship between letters and sounds and letters and meanings to assist in the identification of known words and to independently figure out unfamiliar words. Research evidence tends to favor explicit phonics. However, the "ideal" phonics program would probably incorporate features from implicit phonics as well. The Commission believes that the approaches to phonics recommended in programs available today fall considerably short of the ideal, and we call for renewed efforts to improve the quality of instructional design, materials, and teaching strategies.

The right maxims for phonics are: Do it early. Keep it simple. Except in cases of diagnosed individual need, phonics instruction should have been completed by the end of the second grade.

Phonics and Reading Selections for the Beginning Reader

No matter how children are introduced to words, very early in the program they should have experience with reading these words in meaningful texts. The discussion in this section is about the relationship between what children are learning about phonics and the selections they read in their primers.[67] Selections in primers are typically very short and written with a limited set of words.[68] Selections for older students who have acquired basic reading skill are considered in the chapter on Extending Literacy. Obviously, these selections are longer and more complex than those in primers.

Writing the first selections a child will read is a difficult balancing act. Ideally, the selections will be interesting (so that students will *want* to read them), comprehensible (so that students are able to *understand* them), and instructive (so that students will *learn* from them). But

No matter how children are introduced to words, very early in the program they should have experience with reading these words in meaningful texts.

43

how can selections be made interesting when most of the children don't know how to read very many words? How can stories be comprehensible when they must be written with a severely limited set of words? How can selections be instructive so as to most effectively provide students with the opportunity to practice what they are being taught, and at the same time be interesting and comprehensible?

The reality is, that because the number of words that beginners can identify is still very limited, the few short sentences in the earliest school reading selections cannot, in themselves, tell complete stories. Meaning must be constructed not only from the few meager sentences, but also from picture clues and information provided by the teacher or elicited from the children during discussion. This is one of the reasons why early reading lessons are so full of pictures and intervening discussion.

As will be detailed in the next section on Comprehension and the Beginning Reader, the manner in which programs and individual teachers handle early reading lessons is not always optimum. In the meantime, the point is that from the very beginning children should be given *all* of the elements necessary for constructing meaning. This is important because reading at this early level is a new enterprise, and children must be made aware that reading is always directed toward meaning.

Each encounter with a reading selection should serve the dual goals of advancing children's skill at word identification *and* helping them to understand that reading is a process not simply of word recognition, but one of bringing ideas to mind. There is a reciprocal relationship between word identification and comprehension. The selections written for children to read in school should exploit this relationship. As skill at word identification grows, a larger number of printed words becomes accessible to the young reader. As the number of accessible words increases, more coherent and interesting texts come within reach of the child. More coherent texts contain more clues to pronunciation and meaning which, in turn, leads to more fluent word identification.

From the very beginning children should be given *all* of the elements necessary for constructing meaning. This is important because reading at this early level is a new enterprise, and children must be made aware that reading is always directed toward meaning.

There are methods for introducing children to reading that begin with more natural selections that do comprise complete stories. These methods, which will be lumped under the label "whole language" approaches, were briefly sketched in the section on Reading Instruction in Kindergarten (see pp. 28) It is noteworthy that these approaches are used to teach children to read in New Zealand, the most literate country in the world, a country that experiences very low rates of reading failure.[69] However, studies of whole language approaches in the United States have produced results that are best characterized as inconsistent. In the hands of very skillful teachers, the results can be excellent. But the average result is indifferent when compared to approaches typical in American classrooms, at least as gauged by performance on first- and second-grade standardized reading achievement tests.[70]

In the typical American basal reading program, selections in primers are written using sets of words chosen according to one of two criteria: 1) useful words that appear with great frequency in the language and are thus likely to be in young children's listening and speaking vocabularies; or 2) words that exemplify the letter-sound relationships being introduced in phonics instruction.

To illustrate the difference depending upon which of these two criteria are used, the following are the first several sentences from a little story that would be read by typical first graders in approximately November.

> "We have come, Grandma," said Ana.
> "We have come to work with you."
> "Come in," Grandma said.
> "Look in the book," said Grandma.
> "Mix this and this."[71]

In this 26 word excerpt, there are 17 different words. Of these 17, only 3 could be decoded entirely on the basis of letter-sound relationships that have been introduced in the program's phonics lessons.

Now consider the following few sentences of a story from a different program that would also be read in about November of first grade.

Ray loads the boat.
He says, "I'll row."
Neal says, "We'll both row."
They leave, and Eve rides home alone.[72]

Of the 18 different words in this 20 word excerpt, 17 could be decoded entirely on the basis of letter-sound relationships that students should know from the program's phonics lessons. Notice, though, that this selection contains a few words, such as *loads* and *row,* that are a little less likely to be known by some first graders than the words in the first selection, and perhaps somewhat less useful in reading later selections.

Both these programs teach phonics. At the point where the children would read the selections excerpted above, both have introduced about 30 letter-sound relationships. But only the second program gives the child a good opportunity to use phonics in actual reading.

Phonics instruction is just the first step toward the ultimate goal of fast, accurate word identification and fluent reading. What must occur is that students become so familiar with letter-sound relationships that words are identified automatically, that is, with little conscious attention. This will happen more readily when students encounter in the materials they are reading words that embody the letter-sound relationships that are being taught.

An analysis of eight basal reading series has indicated, however, that there is little connection between the phonics lessons and the reading selections in the primers of the best-selling programs.[73] Phonics is poorly integrated because these programs introduce the most important and useful familiar words first. The problem is that there is an irregular relationship between the spelling and the pronunciation of many of the most useful, familiar words. Consider, for instance, *said* and *come.* If they were regular, *said* would rhyme with *raid* and *come* would rhyme with *home.*

There has been a traditional sequence for introducing letter-sound relationships in phonics lessons. Briefly, children are taught consonant sounds, then short vowel sounds, then long vowel sounds in regular words such as *bake* and *kite*. When programs using this sequence seek perfect regularity between spelling and pronunciation, using only letter-sound relationships that have already been taught, the result can be selections for beginning readers comprised of deadly sentences such as, "Dan had a tan fan." Children do not require this much regularity to master the alphabetic principle. One key to writing more meaningful selections for young readers may be more flexibility in the choice of the order for teaching letter-sound relationships. Relationships could be introduced in an order that makes accessible the largest possible vocabulary of useful words.

The important point is that a high proportion of the words in the earliest selections children read should conform to the phonics they have already been taught. Otherwise they will not have enough opportunity to practice, extend, and refine their knowledge of letter-sound relationships. However, a rigid criterion is a poor idea. Requiring that, say, 90 percent of the words used in a primer must conform to letter-sound relationships already introduced would destroy the flexibility needed to write interesting, meaningful stories. What the field of reading does not need is another index that gets applied rigidly. What the field does need is an understanding of the concepts at work.

Is it possible to write interesting, comprehensible, and natural-sounding selections for young readers while at the same time constraining the vocabulary on the basis of letter-sound relationships? The answer is that it ought to be possible to come much closer to the ideal than the most widely-used programs do at the present time. The following guidelines may help: First, letter-sound relationships can be introduced in a sequence that would allow early use of as rich as possible a set of words while still exemplifying the alphabetic principle. Second, selections can include some useful irregular words without confusing children. Third, selections can include some regular words that embody letter-sound relationships that haven't been introduced yet, but are needed to make interesting, meaningful stories. Again, while it is

The important point is that a high proportion of the words in the earliest selections children read should conform to the phonics they have already been taught.

essential that authors of primers have flexibility, a fairly high proportion of the words must conform to already-taught letter-sound relationships if phonics instruction is to have substantial value.

Children have an easier time understanding stories written in familiar language. Familiarity of language involves not only the familarity of words but also the familiarity of sentence structures. Children, and indeed, most readers, have a difficult time understanding sentences written in styles that they don't frequently hear or use. Even the speech of first-grade children is much more sophisticated than that in basal readers. First-grade children do not say "The cat is there. See the cat. It is black." More likely, a first-grade child would say, "There's a black cat over there." Research has suggested that when children are given a text that conforms to their speech patterns, they comprehend it better.[74]

Writing the first selections a child will read is "a difficult balancing act," to be sure. But there are examples of selections for young readers that meet the technical requirements for a controlled vocabulary and at the same time tell a story and use language in artful ways. One notable example is *Green Eggs and Ham* written by the famous children's author, Dr. Seuss.[75] Large publishing companies invest upward of $15,000,000 to bring out new basal reading programs. Within budgets of this size, surely it is possible to hire gifted writers who can create stories far superior to the standard fare. The Commission believes that the American people ought to expect and should demand better reading primers for their children.

Comprehension and Beginning Reading

The heart of reading instruction in American classrooms is the small group reading lesson in which the teacher works with some children while the rest complete assignments at their seats. This is the usual arrangment in first, second, and third grade, and sometimes beyond. The small group lesson provides the opportunity for instruction and practice on all aspects of reading. For

Large publishing companies invest upward of $15,000,000 to bring out new basal reading programs. Within budgets of this size, surely it is possible to hire gifted writers who can create stories far superior to the standard fare.

the beginning reader, it is a major opportunity to acquire insights into comprehension and to link word identification and comprehension.

The typical teacher's major resource on how to conduct this lesson is the manual that is part of the commercial reading program the school district has purchased. The teacher's manual contains detailed suggestions for conducting every lesson, often in as much detail as the script for a play. Presented in bold type within the manual is the exact wording of statements that the teacher can make to students. For example, to begin a lesson the manual may suggest that the teacher say, "Today we're going to read a story about polar bears. Have any of you ever seen a polar bear in a zoo?" Further directions will then be given in plain type such as "Give children several moments to discuss polar bears. After that, read the introductory statement about the story."

Some school districts afford teachers the option of using any of a variety of materials and approaches to teach reading. More typical, though, is the district that requires the use of the basal reading program that it has purchased. Even these districts usually give teachers flexibility in whether or not they follow the teacher's manual word for word. Classroom observation and interviews with teachers suggest that, whether by choice or not, most teachers do rely on manuals.[76] The teachers' manuals that accompany the best-selling commercial reading programs suggest lessons with three basic parts: preparation, reading, and discussion.

Preparation. In the preparation phase, the teacher is supposed to introduce the new words that will be encountered in the day's basal reader selection and make sure the children possess the background knowledge required to understand the story. The preparation phase is one place where an aspect of comprehension may be explicitly taught or, in the primary grades, where phonics may be taught. The preparation phase may conclude with the teacher's stating a purpose or asking a question to guide reading.

Systematic classroom observation reveals that prepa-

Classroom observation and interviews with teachers suggest that, whether by choice or not, most teachers do rely on manuals.

49

ration for reading is the phase of the small group lesson that is most often slighted, or even skipped altogether.[77] Thus, as a rule, little focused attention is given to developing the background knowledge that will be required to understand the day's story. This is a topic on which teachers' manuals do include specific recommendations. When asked why they neither follow the recommendations in the manuals nor substitute instruction of their own design, teachers say they don't have the time.[78]

Several studies indicate that using instructional time to build background knowledge pays dividends in reading comprehension.[79] It must be warned, though, that there has been a rush of enthusiasm for this practice in professional circles. Teachers are receiving all manner of suggestions waving the banner of background knowledge, some of which may, indeed, be a waste of time. Teachers are being urged to engage children in activities and discussion that may range over too wide an array of topics.

Useful approaches to building background knowledge prior to a reading lesson focus on the concepts that will be central to understanding the upcoming story, concepts that children either do not possess or may not think of without prompting. The advice in teachers' manuals is often unfocused, as in the polar bear example at the beginning of this section.[80] Unstructured preparation may wander away from the concepts of central importance.

The effect of preparation for reading on children's recall of a story was examined in a study which compared unfocused preparation with preparation that highlighted the central ideas of the story.[81] The plot of the story involved a woman who wishes on a star, a raccoon who comes nightly to her doorstep to look for food, and some bandits. The raccoon's masked appearance frightens the bandits into dropping a bag of money, which the raccoon picks up and eventually drops at the woman's doorstep on his nightly search for food. Finding the money, the woman attributes it to her wish on a star.

> Useful approaches to building background knowledge prior to a reading lesson focus on the concepts that will be central to understanding the upcoming story, concepts that children either do not possess or may not think of without prompting.

The suggested steps for preparation in the teacher's manual led to a discussion of raccoons as clever, playful animals. Yet to understand the story, children must grasp the ideas of coincidence and habit, since the raccoon's habitual behavior allows the coincidences to occur. Children who received preparation that concentrated on these ideas did much better in remembering the central ideas of the story than children prepared according to the suggestions in the teacher's manual.[82]

Much of the research showing that it is essential for children to learn to construct meaning based on background knowledge, as well as information in the text, has been conducted recently. This probably explains the low priority this aspect of reading receives in most classrooms today. Teachers, principals, and reading supervisors are just now getting the opportunity to learn about the research and adjust their priorities.

Reading. The second phase of a typical lesson is reading the day's selection. A basic issue is the proper role for silent and oral reading considering the children's age and ability. Frequent opportunities to read aloud make sense for the beginning reader. In the first place, oral reading makes a tie with the experience children have had of reading in their homes, nursery schools, and kindergartens as adults have read to them. Further, oral reading makes observable aspects of an otherwise unobservable process, providing teachers with a means for checking progress, diagnosing problems, and focusing instruction. Not to be underestimated is the function oral reading serves in providing young children a way to share their emerging ability with their parents and others.

Nor should oral reading be discarded altogether once children are fairly skilled readers. Opportunities to read aloud and listen to others read aloud are features of the literate environment, whatever the reader's level. There is no substitute for a teacher who reads children good stories. It whets the appetite of children for reading, and provides a model of skillful oral reading. It is a practice that should continue throughout the grades. Choral reading of poetry and reading plays also

> There is no substitute for a teacher who reads children good stories. It whets the appetite of children for reading, and provides a model of skillful oral reading. It is a practice that should continue throughout the grades.

contribute to oral reading skill and help keep oral traditions alive. However, as the reader moves beyond the initial stages of literacy, more time will be devoted to silent reading, since that is the form that skilled reading most often takes.

Current observations of American classrooms indicate that teachers do differentiate the amount of oral and silent reading according to the reader's level. A study of 600 reading-group sessions found that low-ability readers at the first-grade level read orally during about 90% of the time allocated to the lesson, while high-ability first-graders read aloud about 40% of the time. By Grade 5, low-ability groups spent somewhat over 50% of lesson time reading aloud whereas high-ability groups averaged less than 20%.[83]

The way oral reading is handled in the typical classroom may not be optimum. Authorities recommend that children read a selection silently before they read it aloud. Research suggests that this practice improves oral reading fluency.[84] However, classroom observations reveal that silent reading before oral reading is frequently omitted,[85] which is like being asked to perform a play without having read the script beforehand. Consequently, unless the children are already rather good readers, the reading is unnecessarily slow and halting, and the experience may be needlessly stressful for some children.

The value of oral reading depends in part on the way the teacher deals with mistakes. If a child makes a large number of mistakes, this usually means that the selection is too difficult and that the child ought to be moved to an easier one. Otherwise, a sensible rule of thumb is to ignore most mistakes unless the mistake disrupts the meaning of the text. Even professional oral readers, such as radio and TV announcers, frequently deviate from the text in small ways. When a teacher is compulsive about always correcting small mistakes, the child's train of thought will be interrupted.

Some teachers pay too much attention to correcting what they judge to be imperfections in the pronunciation of children, and thereby may interfere with compre-

The value of oral reading depends in part on the way the teacher deals with mistakes. A sensible rule of thumb is to ignore most mistakes unless the mistake disrupts the meaning of the text.

hension. Overemphasis on standard pronunciation can be a serious problem when the child is not a native speaker of English or the child speaks a different dialect of English than the teacher. For instance, in one study a lesson was observed in which the children were reading a selection that contained the word *garbage*.[86] The white teacher interrupted a black child several times trying to get him to say /garrrbage/ instead of /gahbage/.

When a child makes an oral reading mistake that changes the meaning, the best technique is to first wait and see whether the child can come up with the right word without help. If not, the teacher should direct the child's attention to clues about the word's pronunciation or meaning, depending upon the nature of the error. When the word has been correctly identified, the child should be encouraged to reread the sentence. This helps to assure that the child assimilates the correction and can recover the meaning of the whole sentence. Research suggests that teachers who deal with oral reading errors in the manner that has just been outlined produce larger-than-average gains in reading achievement.[87] Teachers who routinely supply the correct word, or permit other children in the group to call out the correct word, get children in the habit of waiting passively for help.

When children read orally, it is most often in a format called "round robin reading." Each child in a reading group takes a turn reading aloud several lines or a page of the story. An issue in round robin reading is equal distribution of turns for reading among the children. When a teacher always calls on volunteers, it has been shown that assertive children get more than their share of turns. This is undesirable because there is evidence that the child reading aloud and directly receiving instruction from the teacher is getting more from the lesson than the children who are following along.[88] A simple method for equalizing opportunity is to move around the group giving each child a turn in order. This method has produced good results in several studies.[89]

A problem with round robin reading is that the quality

No one would expect a novice pianist to sight read a new selection every day, but that is exactly what is expected of the beginning reader.

of practice is often poor. This problem is acute in the low-ability group where children hear only other poor readers stumbling over words. This problem can be lessened by having the children read the selection silently beforehand. [See also the section on grouping in the Teacher and the Classroom chapter.]

Even under the best of circumstances, round robin reading is not ideal for developing fluency and comprehension. An alternative technique that has proved successful in small-scale tryouts is to have children repeatedly read the same selections until an acceptable standard of fluency is attained. This can be done in several ways: Small groups can read along with an adult or they can follow a tape-recorded version; they can practice silently and then read aloud to the teacher; pairs of children can take turns reading aloud to one another. Poor readers who engage in repeated reading show marked improvement in speed, accuracy, and expression during oral reading of new selections and, more important, improvement in comprehension during silent reading.[90] Repeated reading deserves consideration as an alternative to the conventional practice of having children read aloud new material every day. No one would expect a novice pianist to sight read a new selection every day, but that is exactly what is expected of the beginning reader.

In addition to oral reading, children of every age and ability ought to be doing more extended silent reading. The amount of time children spend reading silently in school is associated with year-to-year gains in reading achievement.[91] Even young readers benefit from opportunities for silent reading. For instance, increased silent reading for beginners is one of the features of a very successful program for low-income Hawaiian children who are otherwise at risk for educational failure.[92] [See also the section on independent reading in the chapter on Extending Literacy.]

To summarize, classroom time spent on either oral or silent reading is time well spent. Even beginning readers should do more silent reading. They should usually read silently before they are asked to read aloud

Children of every age and ability ought to be doing more extended silent reading.

Getting the most from the customary practice of round robin oral reading requires the teacher to distribute turns equally among the children, skillfully handle mistakes, and focus attention on meaning. But alternatives to round robin reading of new material, such as repeated reading, appear to hold more promise for promoting reading fluency and comprehension.

Discussion. Following the reading of a selection, the final phase of a typical reading lesson is discussion. In the primary grades, there are brief discussions after each section of the selection and a longer discussion when the whole story has been completed. In the intermediate grades, the interspersed discussion periods are not usually present. The discussion phase is a place where the teacher may provide direct instruction in some aspect of reading comprehension, using the day's selection for illustration. In the primary grades, this is the point where phonics instruction is usually provided. The last thing the teacher does is explain the seatwork assignment and make sure the children understand what they are supposed to do before they return to their seats.

A clear finding from research of the past decade is that young readers, and poor readers of every age, do not consistently see relationships between what they are reading and what they already know.[93] Research also establishes that questions asked during the discussion phase of a lesson are a useful tool for helping children see relationships. Questions that lead children to integrate information about the central points of a selection with their prior knowledge significantly enhance reading comprehension.[94]

Classroom research indicates that teachers make heavy use of manuals when leading discussions.[95] Manuals include a large number of questions for each story, and most of them are asked during a typical lesson. While research verifies that asking well-crafted questions can be an important means of promoting comprehension, analysis of the questions in manuals reveals many that are poorly crafted — too general, leading the children's

> A clear finding from research of the past decade is that young readers, and poor readers of every age, do not consistently see relationships between what they are reading and what they already know.

55

thinking afield; or trivial, focusing their thinking on unimportant details.[96]

Questions are a means of conveying to students the points they should be attempting to understand as they read future selections as well as a means for checking to see that they have understood the selection they have just read. Thus, questions following a story should probe the major elements of the plot. If the story has a moral, discussion should bring out this deeper meaning.

No piece of advice about questioning has been repeated more often than the proscription, "Don't ask too many detail questions." For instance, if a story were to say that Sally was wearing a red dress, teachers may be warned against asking about the color of her dress. This advice is incomplete, however. The question is perfectly sensible if the color of Sally's dress figures in the plot. A more complete statement about questions is that, as a general rule, they should be formulated to motivate children's higher-level thinking. When questions about details are asked, usually they should be links in a chain of questions that lead to an inference about a hard-to-understand part of the passage or an understanding of the selection as a whole.

While questions during the preparation and discussion phases of a reading lesson are important, these do not substitute for active, direct instruction. In direct instruction, the teacher explains, models, demonstrates, and illustrates reading skills and strategies that students ought to be using.[97] There is evidence that direct instruction produces gains in reading achievement beyond those that are obtained with only less direct means such as questions.[98] [More is said about direct instruction in the chapter on Extending Literacy.]

The emphasis during reading lessons should be on understanding and appreciating the content of the story. Lessons in which the children do little else but take turns reading the story, and the teacher does little else but correct reading errors, are ineffective. Teachers should periodically ask students questions that lead them to understand the critical points of the story. As needed, the teacher should explain points that students have

The emphasis during reading lessons should be on understanding and appreciating the content of the story. Lessons in which the children do little else but take turns reading the story, and the teacher does little else but correct reading errors, are ineffective.

confused or demonstrate skills that students should be using.

In conclusion:

- **Parents play roles of inestimable importance in laying the foundation for learning to read.** Parents should informally teach preschool children about reading and writing by reading aloud to them, discussing stories and events, encouraging them to learn letters and words and teaching them about the world around them. These practices help prepare children for success in reading.

- **Parents have an obligation to support their children's continued growth as readers.** In addition to laying a foundation, parents need to facilitate the growth of their children's reading by taking them to libraries, encouraging reading as a free time activity, and supporting homework.

- **Kindergarten programs should emphasize oral language and writing as well as the beginning steps in reading.** Reading builds on oral language facility, concepts about the functions of printed language and a desire to communicate through writing, as well as specific knowledge about letters and words.

- **Phonics instruction improves children's ability to identify words.** Useful phonics strategies include teaching children the sounds of letters in isolation and in words, and teaching them to blend the sounds of letters together to produce approximate pronunciations of words. Another strategy that may be useful is encouraging children to identify words by thinking of other words with similar spellings. Phonics instruction should go hand in hand with opportunities to identify words in meaningful sentences and stories. Phonics should be taught early and kept simple.

- **Reading primers should be interesting, comprehensible and instructive.** To be most instructive, primers must contain many words that can be identified using phonics that has already been taught. There is a natural relationship between word identification and comprehension. Primer selections should be written to exploit this relationship. After the earliest selections, primers should tell complete, interesting stories.

- **Both oral and silent reading are important for the beginner.** Children should read selections silently before they are asked to read them orally. Getting the most from oral reading requires the teacher to distribute turns for reading equally, skillfully handle mistakes, and keep the emphasis on meaning.

- **Reading lessons should stress understanding and appreciating the content of the selection.** Discussions before reading and discussions and questioning after reading should motivate children's higher level thinking, with an emphasis on making connections with their prior knowledge of the topic. In addition to asking questions, teachers should directly instruct children in skills and strategies that help them become better readers.

*As proficiency develo[...]
reading should be th[...]
not so much as a se[...]
subject in school but [...]
integral to learning [...]
literature, social studies,
and science.*

Extending Literacy

Children still have much to learn about reading even when they can decode words with a fair degree of facility and can understand simple, well-written stories. Increasingly, though, as proficiency develops reading should be thought of not so much as a separate subject in school but as integral to learning literature, social studies, and science.

Even for beginners, reading should not be thought of simply as a "skill subject." It is difficult to imagine, for instance, that kindergarteners could be called literate for their age if they did not know *Goldilocks and the Three Bears* or *Peter Rabbit.* For each age, there are fables, fairy tales, folk tales, classic and modern works of fiction and nonfiction that embody the core of our cultural heritage. A person of that age cannot be considered literate until he or she has read, understood, and appreciated these works.[1]

This chapter deals with three essential factors that influence whether the young readers will be able to extend their skill to meet the challenges of subject matter learning. The first is the quality of school textbooks. The second is the nature of the instruction that teachers provide. The third is opportunities for meaningful practice.

School Textbooks

Authors and editors face many pressures as they prepare the selections that comprise basal readers and write the textbooks intended for older children who have acquired the rudiments of reading skill. The criteria for vocabulary control that must figure in the design of primers are supplemented and then replaced by other criteria as the selections get longer. The selections must reflect classic literary traditions. At the same time some selections must be "timely" so that modern students will relate to them. Selections on history, geography, and science must be accurate and informative. To these criteria are added the demands of special interest groups seeking to influence the topics that will be presented in schoolbooks and the way in which these topics are handled.

The remainder of this section deals with two of the most pressing and important issues in writing school textbooks. The first is controlling the difficulty and appropriateness of textbooks. The second is designing the bridges that help young readers make the transition from simple stories to more complicated reading material.

Controlling the Difficulty of Schoolbooks

A vexing problem for textbook writers is matching the difficulty level of the material to the ability level of the child for whom the material is intended. It is obvious that *Pride and Prejudice* is unsuitable for a seven-year-old. But it is much less obvious just what material would have a suitable level of difficulty for a child of this age. Educators have long wanted a simple, objective method for determining an appropriate difficulty level for schoolbooks. In response, several decades of research and development have been invested in easy-to-use methods. The result is what are called "readability formulas."

The formulas now in use encompass two features of written language: The length of the sentences, expressed as an average in a sample of a book's text; and, the complexity of the words used, also expressed as an average (in number of unfamiliar words, or number of syllables) in a sample of the text.

An example of how one common readability formula is applied to a passage is as follows.[2] Three sample passages of 100 words each are randomly selected from a reading selection. For each passage, the number of words per sentence and the number of syllables per word are computed. These figures are averaged over the three samples to give an estimate of the sentence length and an estimate of the word length for the entire selection. All that remains is to refer to a graph, plotting word length on one side of the graph and sentence length on the other. The point of intersection on the graph gives the approximate grade level for which material is appropriate, without actually having to insert the numbers into a formula and perform any calculations. For example, a story with an average sentence length of 14 words and an average word length of 1.24 syllables is estimated to be appropriate for a typical child in the fifth grade. If the sentences averaged only 12 words and the word length was 1.24, the material would be estimated as appropriate for an average child in the fourth grade.

As this illustration indicates, readability formulas are easy to apply. The formulas also give a fairly good prediction of how difficult typical students will find a book.[3] For these reasons schools have come to depend on readability formulas to appraise the difficulty and appropriateness of schoolbooks. Most schools will not purchase material that does not satisfy one of the formulas.

To sell their textbooks, publishing companies face a temptation to "write to formula." However, this is a purpose for which the formulas were never intended. As one authority on readability has admonished, "merely shortening words and sentences to improve readability is like holding a lighted match under a thermometer when you want to make your house warmer."[4]

Important features of text, such as the logical organization of ideas and the clarity of sentence structures, don't show up in the measurements taken to calculate

A vexing problem for textbook writers is matching the difficulty level of the material to the ability level of the child for whom the material is intended.

readability. It is quite possible to write a disorganized text, full of incomprehensible sentences, and still achieve a desired readability score.[5] Indeed, dividing long sentences into shorter sentences and substituting familiar words for less familiar words can make a text *more* difficult to understand. This seeming contradiction is easy to explain. When a long sentence is divided into shorter sentences, a reader often has to make more inferences. This is because words that connect ideas such as *so, because,* and *since* in long sentences are omitted when the sentence is divided. For example, compare the following passages in which an original text has been rewritten to conform to a readability formula:

(original)
Little Hippo was the pet of the herd. Every morning the big hippos waited for him to wake up so they could take care of him.

(rewritten)
Every morning was the same for Little Hippo. All the big hippos would wait for him to get up. They wanted to take care of him.[6]

To reduce sentence length, a compound sentence has been broken into two simple sentences by deleting the conjunction *so.* But the connection between the two pieces of information is now left vague. Consequently, the reader has to infer that the big hippos were eager for Little Hippo to wake up *because* they enjoyed taking care of him.

Similarly, substituting familiar words for less familiar words to conform to a readability formula can also make a text more difficult to understand. When a common word is substituted for a less common word, the common word may be less informative. A reader may have fewer clues to the meaning originally intended by the author. For example:

(original)
One morning Little Hippo felt cross. 'I don't want lily pads and corn,' he grumbled. 'I wish the hippos wouldn't watch everything I do.'

(rewritten)
One morning Little Hippo said to himself, 'I don't

want anyone to bring me food.' 'I don't want anyone
to take care of me.'[7]

In the rewritten version, *said to himself* has been substituted for *felt cross* and *grumbled, food* for *lily pads and corn,* and *take care of me* for *watch everything I do.* Although it contains fewer uncommon words, the rewritten passage is vague and no longer communicates the idea in the original that Little Hippo wants privacy and something different for breakfast. For no apparent reason, Little Hippo now rejects food and care in general.

These contrasting passages illustrate that reducing sentence length and changing word familiarity does not necessarily produce more comprehensible text. They also illustrate that the verve and style of an original can be lost in translation.

In summary, readability formulas are useful as a first check on the difficulty and appropriateness of books. However, no formula gauges the clarity, coherence, organization, interest, literary quality, or subject matter adequacy of books. Inevitably, overreliance on readability formulas by the schools and their misuse by the publishing industry has contributed to bad writing in schoolbooks. The Commission urges those who buy books and those who write and edit them to supplement analyses using readability formulas with analyses of the deeper factors that are essential for quality.

The Transition to Literature, Social Studies, and Science

Formal reading instruction begins with very simple stories. Eventually the young reader must develop the skill to understand literature and subject matter textbooks. This transition can be made easier through careful selection of material, coherent writing, and sound editing.

There are good reasons why reading instruction begins with simple stories. One is the need to control vocabulary. A deeper and more subtle reason is that children readily acquire an understanding of the whole structure of stories and, therefore, stories are especially comprehensible to children.

Story "structure" refers to the way in which ideas in a story are connected. Well-formed children's stories place characters in settings. The characters have goals that are expressly stated or easily inferable. The characters make plans and undertake actions to achieve those goals. The actions unfold in an orderly sequence. There are outcomes in a well-formed story. Sometimes the characters fail and sometimes they succeed in reaching their goals, but in any case they have emotional reactions to these outcomes.

Research has shown that most children's sense of the structure of stories develops rapidly.[8] By the time children who have *heard* a lot of stories enter elementary school, they have a surprisingly sophisticated understanding of story structure. They know about characters, plot, action, and resolution. How does a knowledge of story structure make it easier for children to understand the stories in their readers? Research with young children reveals that the more closely a story fits an expected structure, the easier it is for a reader to grasp and remember the important ideas.[9] Stories that conform to a "good" story structure make it easier for readers to connect the parts of the story.

Regrettably, many stories for the early grades do not have a predictable structure.[10] This is especially true of the stories in primers and first-grade basal readers. In fact many of these selections do not actually tell a story, as was illustrated in the chapter on Emerging Literacy. This makes the selections less comprehensible, less interesting, and probably slows progress in learning to read.

Later selections generally do tell a story, but they often fail to have a structure that is as clear and comprehensible as possible. A pervasive fault is that stories written or edited for use in the primary grades do not give enough insight into characters' goals, problems, motives, plans, and feelings.[11] This can make the plot difficult to figure out. The following paragraph about a raccoon is from a second-grade story:

> Because he [the raccoon] was still hungry, he started to look for something more to eat. Just as he started

Many stories for the early grades do not have a predictable structure. In fact many of these selections do not actually tell a story.

to look, he heard something coming down the road. Two men came along on their horses. The raccoon hid in back of a tree.[12]

As this paragraph is written, the raccoon's motivation for hiding may not be clear, and the animal's action may seem arbitrary. If the last sentence is changed to, "Because wild animals are afraid of people, the raccoon hid in back of a tree." the paragraph becomes easier for a child to understand.[13]

Obviously, as students advance they will have to learn to cope with texts in which both the structure and content are unfamiliar. Somewhat different demands are imposed by the two major types of texts the maturing reader faces — literature and subject matter textbooks.

With respect to literature, students must be able to understand increasingly complicated plots and characterization. They need to be able to cope with literature in which devices such as flashbacks and flash-forwards are frequent and subtle in realization. They need to be able to appreciate the moral or author's point as well as how the plot is resolved. Particularly in the early grades, made-for-school stories are not as complex as the literature intended for children in the same grades on the shelves of libraries and bookstores.[14] This fact has caused some authorities to wonder whether school reading programs adequately prepare children for genuine literature.

Subject matter textbooks pose the biggest challenge for young readers being weaned from a diet of simple stories.[15] Most selections in basal readers for the primary grades are stories. It is only common sense that children would be helped to make the transition to textbooks if early basal readers contained more high-quality nonfiction. Though there is little hard evidence on the point, anyone experienced in working with young readers knows that they can understand and do appreciate selections on such topics as animals, clouds, and how to make a kite, provided the material is presented in a coherent fashion.

Compared to simple stories, the intrinsic structure in a field such as geography does less to guide an author's

Subject matter textbooks pose the biggest challenge for young readers being weaned from a diet of simple stories.

67

organization of a text and, later, the student's reading of the text. In other words, the author of a textbook chapter has many more options about which topics to include and the order in which they are addressed than the author of a simple story. For instance, while there is an underlying structure to geography, it does not dictate that the political boundaries, topography, climate, culture, economy, history, and government of a country must all be discussed. It does not dictate the order in which topics are addressed. It does not dictate which of the possible connections between climate and economy or culture and government must be drawn.

Thus, if a textbook is to be easy to learn from, it must contain signals so that the reader can figure out the organization the author has used. Signaling can be provided by words or phrases that give clues to the structure; for example, the phrases *in contrast* and *on the other hand*. Previews or introductory statements, headings, and summary statements can also provide signals to the reader. Evidence is accumulating that confirms and extends the common sense conclusion that to be effective textbooks must be well-organized.[16]

Above all, textbooks must try to lay bare the fundamental structures of history, geography, health, and science — and in a manner that permits children and youth to grasp the structures.

Above all, textbooks must try to lay bare the fundamental structures of history, geography, health, and science — and in a manner that permits children and youth to grasp the structures.[17] A key to accomplishing this is building on the knowledge students already possess. For instance, a somewhat more abstract version of the structure of simple stories can be harnessed to yield one level of understanding of history.

Throughout history, people have had goals or faced problems, they have developed plans to reach the goals or solve the problems, they have acted on the basis of the plans, and their actions have resulted in outcomes. Though history has its individual "characters," more often than in a simple story the agent in an historical episode is an institution, government, or group of people. Whereas a child reading a story will immediately apprehend the motive of hungry boys ransacking a kitchen in search of the cookie jar, the same child reading about the Westward movement in this country may find the motives of the pioneers more obscure. Still, there is a parallel between the structure of stories and the structure of historical episodes that can be exploited.

Scholars who have examined subject matter textbooks often have failed to discover a logical structure.[18] Sections of many textbooks consist of little more than lists of facts loosely related to a theme. Abrupt, unmotivated transitions are frequent. Textbooks are as likely to emphasize a trivial detail or a colorful anecdote as a fundamental principle.

For instance, in the section of a middle-grade history textbook about the building of the transcontinental railroad, one quarter of the words are used to recount the tale of Governor Leland Stanford who in Promontory, Utah, on May 10, 1869, swung a sledge hammer at a golden spike and missed.[19] A close analysis of the sections from several textbooks on the building of the transcontinental railroad revealed that none of them explained clearly why people in this country wanted to build the railroad, what the plans were for accomplishing the task, or what happened as a consequence of this monumental project.[20] Every textbook went into considerable detail about the actions of the railroad construction crews, but these actions were not linked to goals, plans, and outcomes.

When textbooks make clear the connections between motive and action, form and function, or cause and effect, students understand better. One of a growing body of studies that supports this conclusion dealt with textbook material on the workings of the human circulatory system.[21] The first two paragraphs below are excerpted from a junior high school science textbook. The second two paragraphs are excerpted from a version of the material rewritten to make explicit the connections between the structure and function of each of the major parts of the circulatory system.

(original)

A human heart is a cone-shaped, muscular organ about the size of a large fist. The heart is located in the center of the chest behind the breastbone and between the lungs.

A close analysis of the sections from several textbooks on the building of the transcontinental railroad revealed that none of them explained clearly why people in this country wanted to build the railroad, what the plans were for accomplishing the task, or what happened as a consequence of this monumental project.

69

A human heart contains four chambers — *right atrium (AY tree uhm), left atrium, right ventricle* (VEN trih kuhl), and *left ventricle*. Right and left refer to the body's right and left sides. A wall separates the chambers on the right from the chambers on the left.

(rewritten)

The heart is the part of the circulatory system that pumps blood throughout the body. The heart is located in the center of the chest behind the breastbone and between the lungs. The human heart is suited for pumping because it is a hollow, cone-shaped, muscular organ about the size of a large fist. Being hollow, the heart can easily fill up with blood. Once filled, the heart muscle provides the power necessary for pumping the blood through the body.

A human heart contains four hollow chambers made for receiving and sending blood. The *right atrium* (AY tree uhm), and *right ventricle* (VEN truh kuhl) receive and send blood to the lungs, while the *left atrium*, and *left ventricle* receive and send blood to the rest of the body. (Note that right and left refer to your body's right-hand and left-hand sides.) The right and left sides of the heart are separated by a wall of muscle. This wall keeps blood going to the lungs separate from the blood going to the body.[22]

In a study involving several hundred eighth graders, students who studied the rewritten material learned more about the concepts required to understand the circulatory system than students who studied the original version.[23] Though the excerpt above from the rewritten version is much longer than the related excerpt from the original, the two versions were the same length when considered as a whole. The rewritten version was kept the same length by deleting what was judged to be extraneous information, such as the fact that, "The work done by the heart each minute is about equal to lifting 32 kg a distance of 30 cm off the ground."

In conclusion, many discussions of what may be wrong with textbooks, and what ought to be done to make them right, miss the mark. Pleas to control the "read-

Many discussions of what may be wrong with text-books miss the mark. Pleas to control the "readability" of textbooks confuse the symptoms with the causes. Pleas for high-quality writing are vague. Pleas to make textbooks "harder" are not on the mark, either. People prove every day that it is possible to make unimportant information hard to understand.

ability" of textbooks often confuse symptoms with causes. Pleas for high-quality writing are vague. "Stylish" writing is not always comprehensible writing. Pleas to make textbooks "harder" are not on the mark either. While students do make faster progress when texts offer some challenge, people prove every day that it is possible to make unimportant information hard to understand. Surely, the goal is to write meaty texts, rich with important concepts and information, that at the same time are easy enough to understand.

To put the conclusion in a nutshell, school books should contain *adequate explanations* considering the skill level, knowledge, and reasoning power of the developing reader. What will be an adequate explanation depends upon the grade. In the case of a second-grade story, it may mean explaining why a raccoon is hiding behind a tree. In the case of a fifth-grade history text, it may mean explaining why the United States wanted to build the transcontinental railroad. In the case of an eighth-grade science text, it may mean explaining how the structure of the human heart supports its function.

Teaching That Will Extend Literacy

Textbook writers can make the process of extracting and integrating relevant information from stories and textbooks much easier for school children. However, well-written materials will not do the job alone. Teachers must instruct students in strategies for extracting and organizing critical information from text. This function of the teacher is all the more important since many textbooks are inadequate. Thus, whether children will make rapid or slow progress in becoming skilled readers depends upon the content and method of instruction.

Research has shown that children's learning is facilitated when critical concepts or skills are directly taught by the teacher.[24] The section on phonics in the preceding chapter concluded that breaking the code is easier for children when instruction directly provides information about letter-sound relationships. Similarly, comprehending information in textbooks is easier if students are instructed in strategies that cause them to focus their

> Well-written materials will not do the job alone. Teachers must instruct students in strategies for extracting and organizing critical information from text.

attention on the relevant information, synthesize the information, and integrate it with what they already know. Children should not be left guessing about how to comprehend. In the words of one researcher, "thinking needs to be made public."[25]

Direct instruction needs to be distinguished from questioning, discussion, and guided practice.[26] Direct instruction in comprehension means explaining the steps in a thought process that gives birth to comprehension. It may mean that the teacher models a strategy by thinking aloud about how he or she is going about understanding a passage. The instruction includes information on why and when to use the strategy. Instruction of this type is the surest means of developing the strategic processing that was identified earlier as characteristic of skilled readers.

In one study of direct comprehension instruction, seventh graders who could identify words adequately but displayed poor comprehension were taught four specific strategies to help them monitor their understanding and learning of textbook selections — devising questions about the text, summarizing, predicting what the author was going to say next, and resolving inconsistencies.[27] These strategies were taught by a technique called "reciprocal teaching" in which teacher and children worked together in small groups. First, the teacher gave direct instruction in the four strategies and modeled how to use them — for instance, by thinking aloud about how to formulate an important question about the text and talking about what she found unclear or confusing. Then, each of the students took on the role of the teacher, and asked the rest of the group a question and identified confusing aspects of the text, with the 'real' teacher giving guidance. After several weeks all students improved in answering comprehension questions. They also carried over these new strategies to other academic subjects. When the students were tested two months later, they were still using the strategies.

In another project, third- and fifth-grade children were taught *how* to use such strategies as skimming, *why* the strategies were helpful, and *when* to use them.[28]

Bulletin boards, worksheets, and direct instruction from teachers reinforced the importance of the strategies, along with such metaphors as 'Be a Reading Detective' and 'Road Signs for Reading'. After four months of instruction, a number of different measures revealed significant improvements in students' reading.

The most logical place for instruction in most reading and thinking strategies is in social studies and science rather than in separate lessons about reading. The reason is that the strategies are useful mainly when the student is grappling with important but unfamiliar content. Outlining and summarizing, for instance, make sense only when there is some substantial material to be outlined or summarized. The idea that reading instruction and subject matter instruction should be integrated is an old one in education, but there is little indication that such integration occurs often in practice.

Indeed, it is a surprising fact, but one documented by studies in Canada as well as the United States, that direct comprehension instruction that goes beyond the meanings of individual words is rare any place in the curriculum in ordinary classrooms.[29] In one well-known study, only 45 minutes of comprehension instruction, not counting time spent asking and answering questions, were found during 17,997 minutes of observation in reading and social studies periods in 39 classrooms in 14 school districts.[30]

Why don't more teachers provide direct instruction in reading strategies? According to experts who have analyzed the teachers' manuals accompanying reading, social studies, and science programs, the advice they contain often is too sketchy to be of much help to a teacher who wants to directly teach some aspect of comprehension such as how to formulate the main idea of a passage.[31]

A manual isn't necessary for a teacher to teach in a fashion that "makes thinking public." However, the expectation that teachers can instruct students in these strategies without good manuals assumes that teachers have been trained to provide such instruction. Since most of the research underlying these strategies is rel-

The idea that reading instruction and subject matter instruction should be integrated is an old one in education, but there is little indication that such integration occurs often in practice.

73

atively recent, this assumption is unrealistic. Just as students need instruction in knowing what, when, why, and how to think strategically when reading textbooks, teachers need to be trained in knowing what, when, why, and how to teach comprehension strategies directly.

Practice Appropriate for Extending Literacy

In this section, the important topic of independent practice of reading will be considered. "Independent" means that the student is expected to work alone with a minimum amount of supervision or help from the teacher or others. There are two aspects to independent practice. The first is practice that is intended to strengthen specific skills or concepts. This function is mainly served by workbooks and skill sheets in today's schools. The second is practice that is intended to reinforce the whole act of reading. The major activity that does this is extended silent reading. Also important are extended opportunities for speaking, listening, and, particularly, writing.

Workbooks and Skill Sheets

Students spend up to 70% of the time allocated for reading instruction in independent practice, or "seat-work."[32] This is an hour per day in the average classroom. Most of this time is spent on workbooks and skill sheets. Children spend considerably more time with their workbooks than they do receiving instruction from their teachers.

Publishers say that the demand for seatwork activities is insatiable. To meet the demand, most publishers supply a range of supplementary exercise sheets in addition to workbooks which relate to the basal reading lessons. Many teachers use the exercises of several publishers as well as ones they have prepared themselves. In the course of a school year, it would not be uncommon for a child in the elementary grades to bring home 1,000 workbook pages and skill sheets completed during reading period.

Analyses of workbook activities reveal that many

Students spend up to 70% of the time allocated for reading instruction in independent practice, or "seatwork." This is an hour per day in the average classroom. Most of this time is spent on workbooks and skill sheets.

require only a perfunctory level of reading.[33] Children rarely need to draw conclusions or reason on a high level. Few activities foster fluency, or constructive and strategic reading. Almost none require any extended writing. Instead, responses usually involve filling a word in a blank, circling or underlining an item, or selecting one of several choices. Many workbook exercises drill students on skills that have little value in learning to read. The exercises sometimes have difficult-to-understand directions and confusing art work. A serious problem is that some workbook pages and many skill sheets are poorly integrated with the rest of the reading lesson.

Consider, for example, the following exercise from a second-grade workbook:

> Read each sentence. Decide which consonant letter is used the most. Underline it each time.
> 1. My most important toy is a toy train.
> 2. Nancy, who lives in the next house, has nine cats.
> 3. Will you bring your box of marbles to the party?[34]

It is peculiar to suppose that, if children can already read the sentences, their reading ability will be improved by asking them to underline consonants. Furthermore, though the children are directed to "read each sentence," they don't need to read anything but the directions to do the task. The one certain conclusion is that the exercise is time-consuming and extremely tedious.

Even young children often see the futility of doing workbook page after workbook page. One researcher asked children what they were doing when they were occupied with workbooks.[35] Most saw the pages merely as something to get finished. As one boy, age 6, said, "There! I didn't understand that, but I got it done". Students frequently don't read all the material in worksheets. Instead, they attempt to use shortcuts that allow them to answer in a mechanical fashion. If options *a* and *c* have been used to answer two of three questions, for example, some children will write down *b* for the third question without reading it.

Classroom research suggests that the amount of time

Even young children often see the futility of doing workbook page after workbook page. As one boy, age 6, said, "There! I didn't understand that, but I got it done."

devoted to worksheets is unrelated to year-to-year gains in reading proficiency.[36] Why, then, does this type of seatwork take the largest share of all the time devoted to reading? In the primary grades, the major reason appears to stem from the fact that children are taught reading in small groups. Maintaining the undivided attention of the children in one group is difficult to manage unless the rest of the children are occupied with tasks they can do by themselves that are sure to keep them busy. A contributing reason is the widespread practice of school-mandated tests covering small bits of knowledge about reading. As will be detailed in the chapter on testing, holding teachers responsible for children's performance on these tests reinforces heavy use of seatwork exercises.

In summary, while it cannot be doubted that well-designed workbooks and skill sheets can provide worthwhile practice in aspects of reading, many of these exercise activities are poorly designed. The most notable shortcomings are the dubious value of a large share of the activities to growth in reading proficiency and the lack of integration of the activities with the rest of the reading lesson. For these problems, the publishing industry is responsible. Moreover, in the all too typical classroom, too much of the precious time available for reading instruction is given over to workbook and skill sheet tasks and students invest only the most perfunctory level of attention in the tasks. For these problems, teachers and school administrators are responsible. The conclusion is that workbook and skill sheet tasks should be pared to the minimum that will actually contribute to growth in reading.

Independent Reading

Research suggests that the amount of independent, silent reading children do in school is significantly related to gains in reading achievement.[37] However, the amount of time children spend reading in the average classroom is small. An estimate of silent reading time in the typical primary school class is 7 or 8 minutes per day, or less than 10% of the total time devoted to reading. By the middle grades, silent reading time may average 15 minutes per school day.[38]

Research also shows that the amount of reading students do out of school is consistently related to gains in reading achievement.[39] In one recent study, fifth graders completed a daily log of after-school activities for periods ranging from two to six months.[40] Among all the ways the children reported spending their leisure time, average minutes per day reading books was the best predictor of reading comprehension, vocabulary size, and gains in reading achievement between the second and the fifth grade.

But most children don't read very much during their free time. In the study of fifth graders mentioned above, 50% of the children read books for an average of four minutes per day or less, 30% read two minutes per day or less, and fully 10% never reported reading any book on any day. For the majority of the children, reading from books occupied 1% of their free time, or less. In contrast, the children averaged 130 minutes per day watching TV, or about one third of the time between the end of school and going to sleep.[41]

For the majority of the children, reading from books occupied 1% of their free time, or less.

Increasing the amount of time children read ought to be a priority for both parents and teachers. Reading books (and magazines, newspapers, and even comic books) is probably a major source of knowledge about sentence structure, text structure, literary forms, and topics ranging from the Bible to current events.

Independent reading is probably a major source of vocabulary growth. A synthesis of available evidence suggests that children in grades three through twelve learn the meanings of about 3,000 new words a year.[42] Some of these are directly taught in school, but a moment's reflection will show that this source could account for only a modest proportion of the total. To learn 3,000 words a year would require learning about 15 words every school day. Even the most determined advocates of vocabulary drill do not introduce this many words a day, let alone teach them to the level of mastery. One group of researchers has argued that, beyond the third grade, children acquire the majority of the new words they learn incidentally while reading books and other material.[43]

77

Independent reading is probably a major source of reading fluency. In contrast to workbook pages or computer drills, the reading of books provides practice in the whole act of reading. Practice in this form is likely to be particularly effective in increasing the automaticity of word identification skills. Avid readers do twenty times or more as much independent reading as less frequent readers.[44] This means they are getting vastly more practice and helps to explain why children who read a lot make more progress in reading.

Children who are avid readers come from homes in which reading is encouraged by a parent, grandparent, older brother or sister, or even a baby sitter. They come from homes that have books, subscriptions to children's magazines, and in which both adults and children have library cards.[45] Public and school libraries are especially important for children from poor homes. One study found that the amount of reading children from poor homes did and their gains in reading achievement over the summer were related to the distance they lived from a public library.[46]

Analyses of schools that have been successful in promoting independent reading suggest that one of the keys is ready access to books. However, fully 15% percent of the nation's schools do not have libraries. In most of the remaining schools, the collections are small, averaging just over 13 volumes per student. In 1978, schools that did have libraries were adding less than a book a year per student, which does not even keep up with loss and wear.[47] According to a 1984 evaluation, "the collections of the school library . . are in increasing jeopardy; inventories have been shrinking, and what remains is bordering on the obsolete."[48]

In addition to school-wide libraries, several projects have demonstrated the value of classroom libraries. Children in classrooms with libraries read more, express better attitudes toward reading, and make greater gains in reading comprehension than children who do not have such ready access to books.[49] In one study with non-native English speakers, ample classroom libraries were associated with dramatic improvements in reading

Analyses of schools that have been successful in promoting independent reading suggest that one of the keys is ready access to books. However, fully 15% of the nation's schools do not have libraries. In most of the remaining schools, the collections are small, averaging just over 13 volumes per student.

achievement that were still evident when the children were retested a few years later.[50]

Other features of school programs that are associated with increased independent reading include activities to interest children in books, guidance in choosing books from someone who knows both the books and the children, and time set aside during the school day for independent reading. Research suggests that the frequency with which students read in and out of school depends upon the priority classroom teachers give to independent reading.[51]

The Connection Between Reading and Writing

It cannot be emphasized too strongly that reading is one of the language arts. All of the uses of language — listening, speaking, reading, and writing — are interrelated and mutually supportive. It follows, therefore, that school activities that foster one of the language arts inevitably will benefit the others as well.

Writing activities, in particular, should be integrated into the reading period. Students can do extended writing in place of some of the workbook pages that now occupy so much of their time. Students can write about the material they have just read about in their basal readers. Or they can write about other topics. In either case, writing is seatwork that affects children's reading in positive ways.

Opportunities to write have been found to contribute to knowledge of how written and oral language are related, and to growth in phonics, spelling, vocabulary development, and reading comprehension.[52] Students who write frequently and discuss their writing with others approach reading with what has been termed the "eye of a writer." The following quotation illustrates the change in understanding of one young author:

> Before I ever wrote a book, I used to think there was a big machine, and they typed a title and then the machine went until the book was done. Now I look at a book and I know a guy wrote it and it's been his project for a long time. After the guy writes it, he probably thinks of questions people will ask him and revises it like I do.[53]

In one recent study in grades one, three and five, only 15% of the school day was spent in any kind of writing activity. Two-thirds of the writing that did occur was word for word copying in workbooks. Compositions of a paragraph or more in length are infrequent even at the high school level.

The value for reading is one reason for increased writing. Of course, the principal reason is that learning to write well is a valued goal in its own right. Unfortunately, every recent analysis of writing instruction in American classrooms has reached the same conclusion: Children don't get many opportunities to write. In one recent study in grades one, three and five, only 15% of the school day was spent in any kind of writing activity.[54] Two-thirds of the writing that did occur was word for word copying in workbooks. Compositions of a paragraph or more in length are infrequent even at the high school level.[55]

As was discussed in the chapter on Emerging Literacy, writing can be included in the earliest stages of reading instruction. Young children can write with preformed letters or print labels on pictures. Later, as children gain more control over the physical act of writing, writing ought to become even more integral to reading instruction.

Instruction in grammar is often justified on the grounds that it improves students' writing. In the long run, knowledge of grammar undoubtedly helps people become better writers as well as as better readers and better speakers. However, it is a mistake to suppose that instruction in grammar transfers readily to the actual uses of language. This may be the explanation for the fact that experiments over the last fifty years have shown negligible improvement in the quality of student writing as a result of grammar instruction.[56] Research suggests that the finer points of writing, such as punctuation and subject-verb agreement, may be learned best while students are engaged in extended writing that has the purpose of communicating a message to an audience.[57] Notice that no communicative purpose is served when children are asked to identify on a worksheet the parts of speech or the proper use of *shall* and *will*.

Skillful teachers find ways to give children reasons to communicate to real audiences. Children can retell stories that they have read in the form of a news release for classmates. They can write to maintain classroom life by writing announcements, schedules for class ac-

> **Research suggests that the finer points of writing, such as punctuation and subject-verb agreement, are learned best while students are engaged in extended writing that has the purpose of communicating a message to an audience.**

tivities, diaries of classroom events, records of the weather, and acknowledgments of assistance from school personnel, a parent, or a classroom visitor. Letter writing, in particular, is a form of expression in which there are reasons to write to real audiences.

List writing is an easy way to initiate children into writing. For example, children might read to locate a recipe for cookies to be served at a class party. Once the recipe has been located, newspapers can be studied to determine the best source for ingredients. This could be followed by writing the shopping list of ingredients and directions for making the cookies for the class party.

Another form of writing that has been tried successfully in classrooms is keeping diaries or journals. Some teachers engage in give-and-take with students by periodically writing comments in their journals.[58] These teachers emphasize the content of the children's entries, and are sparing of suggestions about spelling, grammar, or handwriting.

In summary:

- **Readability formulas are useful only as a rough check on the difficulty and appropriateness of books.** It is also important to gauge clarity, organization, interest, literary quality, and subject matter accuracy.

- **School textbooks should be rich with important concepts and information.** Books for all grades need to contain adequate explanations taking into account the skill level, knowledge, and reasoning power of the reader.

- **Teachers need to teach comprehension strategies directly.** Teachers should devote more time to teaching strategies for understanding not only stories but also social studies and science texts.

- **Workbook and skill sheet tasks take too much of the time allotted for reading.** These should be pared to the minimum that will actually contribute to growth in reading.

- **Students should do more extended writing.** Writing is most beneficial when students have a reason to communicate to a genuine audience.

Skillful teachers find ways to give children reasons to communicate to real audiences. Children can retell stories in the form of a news release, they can write announcements, schedules for class activities, diaries of classroom events, records of the weather, and acknowledgments to a classroom visitor.

81

■ **Priority should be given to independent reading.** Two hours a week of independent reading should be expected by the time children are in the third or fourth grade. To do this, children need ready access to books and guidance in choosing appropriate and interesting books. Reading should emphasize works that represent the core of our cultural heritage.

An indisputable conclusion of research is that the quality of teaching makes a considerable difference in children's learning.

The Teacher
and the Classroom

An indisputable conclusion of research is that the quality of teaching makes a considerable difference in children's learning. Studies indicate that about 15 percent of the variation among children in reading achievement at the end of the school year is attributable to factors that relate to the skill and effectiveness of the teacher.[1] In contrast, the largest study ever done comparing approaches to beginning reading found that about 3 percent of the variation in reading achievement at the end of the first grade was attributable to the overall approach of the program.[2] Thus, the prudent assumption for educational policy is that, while there may be some "materials-proof" teachers, there are no "teacher-proof" materials.

Teachers influence children's learning in a number of ways that materials alone cannot. The teacher's critical role in providing direct instruction was discussed in previous chapters. In addition, teachers influence children's learning in the following ways: Managing the classroom environment, pacing and content coverage, and grouping children for instruction.

Management of the Classroom Environment

Teachers who are successful in creating *literate environments* have classrooms that are simultaneously stimulating and disciplined. The successful teacher creates varied opportunities for language use. The successful teacher asks questions that make children think and requires children to answer in ways that communicate ideas clearly. The successful teacher uses language in a manner that sparks children's interest in the meanings and origins of words. In the classrooms of successful teachers, the children are encouraged to ask questions and present information about class experiences, current world events, television programs, and so on. In classrooms that foster enthusiasm for language, the children write a lot and do so for many reasons.

Though writing, speaking, and listening are all important, children must receive reading instruction and have opportunities for reading to become good readers. Research has substantiated that the amount of time that teachers allocate to reading relates to year-to-year gains in reading proficiency, as represented by standardized tests.[3] In the typical American classroom, a great deal of time is allocated to reading instruction. The best available evidence shows that the average is about an hour and a half per day.[4] Depending on the locale, the school day is about five hours in length. Thus, about 30% of the school day in the average classroom is spent in reading instruction. However, it should be reiterated again that much of this time is devoted to workbook pages and skill sheets that have doubtful value in learning to read.

Furthermore, average figures obscure the extremes. The amount of time allocated to reading varies enormously from one classroom to another, even within the same school. Teachers have been observed who allocated as few as 35 minutes per day or as much as 126 minutes per day to reading.[5] At the low end of this range, there is reason to worry that children will not have enough time to make satisfactory progress in reading.

The time allocated to reading may or may not be used efficiently. Thus, more important than time allocated to reading is "engaged time" — the time the child is productively involved in reading.[6] The total amount of engaged time depends on allocated time, of course,

One characteristic that distinguishes effective classrooms from ineffective ones is the teacher's commitment to the belief that all children can learn to read. Effective teachers strive to see that every child masters basic skills and then goes as far beyond this basic level as possible.

and also on the skill of the teacher in managing the class.

Skilled teachers minimize discipline problems, and quickly handle the ones that do arise. At the beginning of the school year, skilled teachers establish routines for potentially time-wasting chores such as making transitions between activities, distributing supplies, getting help with assignments, and turning in completed work. When necessary, they provide instruction in carrying out these routines, and continue to remind students to use the routines until they do so from habit.[7]

Skilled teachers attempt to make clear the purpose of every activity. They make sure children understand how to do each task. They make sure children know what they are supposed to do when they finish a task. In classrooms taught by these teachers, more of the precious time available for learning is spent in activities with academic value.[8]

Effective teachers place a premium on subject matter learning, but they are not indifferent to children as individuals. They are supportive while at the same time maintaining high expectations for learning. One characteristic that distinguishes effective classrooms from ineffective ones is the teacher's commitment to the belief that all children can learn to read. Effective teachers strive to see that every child masters basic skills and then goes as far beyond this basic level as possible.[9]

Pacing and Content Coverage

The pace of instruction strongly predicts year-to-year gains in reading.[10] Children of any given level of ability who are in fast-paced groups show growth beyond the expected. Striking variation is evident across classrooms in the pace at which children move through material. A recent study reported data on the pace of instruction in 60 elementary school classrooms from seven different states.[11] On the average, the high-ability groups in these classrooms covered considerably more running words of text per week than the low-ability groups. The figures were 1100 words as compared to 400 in high- and low-ability first-grade groups and 6,900 as compared to

Striking variation is evident across classrooms in the pace at which children move through material. For instance, the number of words read per week was reported to have varied from 600 to 8,900 in low-ability, fifth-grade groups.

4,400 in high- and low-ability fifth-grade groups. While some differences across grade and ability level are to be expected, the pace of instruction varied by a factor of ten or even twenty within groups at the same grade and supposedly at the same level of ability. For instance, the number of words read per week was reported to have varied from 600 to 8,900 in low-ability, fifth-grade groups.

Of course, the pace of instruction cannot be pushed beyond some limit. In the long run, the pace that can be maintained with a group depends not only on the ability of the children, but on the difficulty of the material, the time allocated to reading, and the percentage of allocated time during which the children remain actively engaged. A time-honored rule is that the pace is optimum when children accurately identify 95% or more of the words in a text while reading aloud. Another rule proposes that children ought to answer about 80% of the teacher's questions satisfactorily. If the level of success falls below these figures, the belief is that the pace is too brisk and the lessons are in danger of floundering. Available evidence does suggest that high levels of success are associated with large year-to-year gains in reading.[12]

Thus, though effective teachers move through material at a brisk pace, they do not sacrifice comprehension. They move in small steps and they move on to the next step only when students have been successful. How the most effective teachers manage to maintain both a fast pace and a high rate of success, two characteristics that may sometimes conflict, is a complex issue that research has not yet completely untangled.

One obstacle to an optimum pace is the meager ration of books with which many classrooms are stocked. There are reports of teachers who slow down when they see that they are running out of material. They may stop reading instruction altogether when they finish the assigned book, since they are not allowed to encroach on next year's book, and either other books are unavailable or the teacher does not perceive that it is important to keep the children reading.

Another obstacle to an optimum pace in some schools is the principal who insists that every child reach certain points in the reading curriculum on specified dates. The result can be that some students are rushed over material without mastering anything while other students mark time.

Grouping for Instruction

When children receive reading instruction in the United States, it usually takes place in a lesson with a small group of children of similar ability. Virtually all primary-grade teachers and many middle-grade teachers divide the children in a class into groups, most often three groups of high-, average-, and low-ability. Reading groups are kept small to make it easier for the teacher to maintain the active engagement of the children. Reading groups are composed on the basis of ability to enable the teacher to adapt the pace of instruction to the children; otherwise, the fast child may be held back or the slow child may be left behind.

In theory, ability grouping allows teachers to pace instruction at a more-nearly-optimum rate for children at every level than would be possible in whole class teaching. In fact, the evidence suggests that ability grouping may improve the achievement of the fast child but not the slow child.[13]

Whatever cute name may be given to a reading group, the children know their place. They evaluate their own abilities on the basis of the status of their group. The low-group students in one school may be at the same reading level as the students in the average group in another school. Yet, the low-group students in the one school may view themselves as poor readers, and their teachers may have lower expectations for their progress.[14]

There are qualitative differences in the experience of children in high and low reading groups that would be expected to place children in low groups at a disadvantage.[15] Children in low groups do relatively more reading aloud and relatively less silent reading. They more often read words without a meaningful context on lists or

> In theory, ability grouping allows teachers to pace instruction at a more-nearly-optimum rate for children at every level than would be possible in whole class teaching. In fact, the evidence suggests that ability grouping may improve the achievement of the fast child but not the slow child.

89

flash cards, and less often read words in stories. Teachers correct a higher proportion of the oral reading mistakes of children in low groups than children in high groups. When a mistake is corrected, teachers are more likely to furnish a clue about pronunciation and less likely to furnish a clue about meaning for children in low groups. Teachers ask relatively more simple, factual questions of children in low groups and relatively fewer questions that require reasoning.

Characteristically, low groups are less engaged with the lesson than high groups.[16] One reason for this is that low groups include children who are low in "social maturity" — that is, children perceived as troublemakers and those who won't pay attention — as well as children who are low in ability. In high groups, the children themselves sometimes police misbehavior and may coach others to pay attention. In low groups, children may distract one another. Moreover, teachers tolerate more interruptions of the lessons of low than high groups.[17]

It is difficult for a child to move from one group to another within a year.[18] Since teachers form the groups at the beginning of the year partly on the basis of the children's standing the previous year, changing groups from one year to the next is also difficult. It is a sad fact but frequently true that, "Once a bluebird, always a bluebird."

Yet the means for assessing reading ability, particularly the ability of children in kindergarten or first grade, are quite fallible. Grouping decisions, therefore, are also fallible. Some scholars have argued that it is not so much ability that determines the future attainment of a young child, but the reading group into which the child is initially placed.[19] As has been detailed already, the child in a group designated as low-ability will receive less instruction and qualitatively different instruction than the child would in a group designated as high-ability. As a result, the child may make slow progress in reading and the initial group designation may become a self-fulfilling prophecy.

A common belief among teachers is that all children

Some scholars have argued that it is not so much ability that determines the future attainment of a young child, but the reading group into which the child is initially placed.

require an equal share of their attention. Though children of all levels require direct instruction from teachers, low-ability children usually do less well than high-ability children when working alone or in small groups without the teacher.[20] In other words, close teacher supervision is particularly important for less able students. Thus, it seems advisable for teachers to assign fewer students to low groups and to keep closer track of these students during independent work periods.

The problems with ability grouping can be alleviated if not eliminated entirely. First, the assignment of children to groups should be reviewed periodically and children switched around, even though this means that some children will not have read all of the previous selections in the book. Second, reading groups do not always have to be formed on the basis of ability. For example, the advantage of small group instruction for holding attention would still be there if children were sometimes grouped on the basis of interest in the topic. Grouping according to interest is feasible, since children usually read at a higher level than may be typical for them when they find the topic particularly interesting.[21] Some reading teachers encourage children to sit in on the lessons of other groups, and report that the "visitors" profit from the experience; this is an idea that other teachers might wish to try. Most important, teachers must take care to provide rich lessons for each group of children, whatever their level.

Because of the serious problems inherent in ability grouping, the Commission believes that educators should explore other options for reading instruction. One option is more use of whole class instruction. This seems feasible for aspects of phonics, spelling, study skills, and comprehension. There are programs that recommend whole class teaching some of the time,[22] and they achieve good results, but whether the results are attributable to the use of whole class instruction or other features of the programs is not known.

Another possible supplement to the conventional arrangement of teacher-led instruction of children grouped according to ability is an arrangement in which children tutor each other, alternating in the role of teacher. "Peer tutoring" has proved successful in arithmetic, and it deserves exploration and study in reading as well.[23]

In conclusion:

- **Effective teachers create literate environments for their children.** They schedule reading and writing activities as a priority, move through materials at an appropriate pace, stimulate and sustain children's attention, and arrange for high rates of success.

- **Grouping by ability may slow the progress of low-ability students.** Both the quantity and quality of instruction for low groups need improvement. Some of the problems with ability grouping can be alleviated by switching group assignments periodically, using criteria other than ability for group assignment, and, maybe, increasing the time devoted to whole class instruction.

Standardized tests of reading comprehension manifestly do not measure everything required to understand and appreciate a novel, learn from a science textbook, or find items in a catalogue.

Testing and Reading Instruction

Tests are as American as apple pie. Most children take at least one reading test a year. Some children take several reading tests a month. Teachers make their own tests, of course, but it is "standardized" tests that receive the most public attention. Standardized tests are commercially published tests that contain a fixed set of items and have uniform procedures for administration and scoring.

Some standardized reading tests are marketed on the basis that they provide diagnostic information about a child's particular strengths and weaknesses. A survey has indicated that, in practice, teachers don't find this information very useful.[1] They report that daily observation of children reading, answering questions, and completing seatwork provides them with more detailed and trustworthy information.

The function that standardized reading tests do serve is to provide objective information about the success of particular children in learning to read and the success of schools in teaching reading. Administrators, school board members, and to a lesser extent teachers, use standardized test scores for these purposes. Parents are also interested in test scores because they appreciate having an assessment of their children's standing that does not depend on the school's grading policy.

The use of standardized tests has increased over the past thirty years.[2] In addition, almost all publishers now sell tests as part of basal reading programs. Many states and some local school districts have mandated minimum competency examinations in reading for entry into or exit from certain grades.

Common Testing Practices

The two general kinds of standardized tests used for measuring reading proficiency in elementary schools are "norm-referenced" and "criterion-referenced" tests.[3] The difference between the two is evident in the labels. Norm-referenced tests use the average performance of other children as the "norm", or reference point, against which an individual's score is evaluated. Criterion-referenced tests focus on the mastery of defined skills or content. An absolute level of performance is set as the criterion against which an individual is evaluated.

Norm-referenced tests measure children's performance in relation to other children in the same grade. Test publishers establish norms based on the performance of representative, nationwide samples of children in each grade. The popular way to report performance on these tests is in terms of "grade equivalents." For instance, a child "reading at the 3.1 level" has obtained a score on a test equivalent to the score that it is estimated the average child would obtain after about one month in the third grade. However, because the relationship between test scores and grade by grade progress in reading is problematic, most authorities prefer another scale, such as the percentile rank, for representing test performance. On a percentile rank scale, the interpretation of performance is straightforward; a child who, for instance, scores at the 88th percentile has done better on the test than 88% of the children in that grade and worse than 12%, give or take a margin of error.

Norm-referenced tests always contain a reading comprehension subtest. This typically consists of a series of brief passages each of which is accompanied by several multiple-choice questions. Nationally normed reading tests usually contain a vocabulary subtest, and may contain subtests on several other aspects of reading as well. These tests can be administered to large groups of children who read silently and mark their answers on special machine-scorable answer sheets.

Criterion-referenced tests are used heavily in schools that employ "skills management systems" for reading instruction. A skills management system works as follows: First, the specific objectives of instruction in an area are established and laid out in a sequence. An instructional objective in reading might be, "The student will be able to identify the referents of pronouns." Then test items are written to assess that ability. One form of the test is given to determine if children need instruction on that skill. If children fail to achieve a level of mastery of 80% or 90% on the pretest, instruction on the skill proceeds. After instruction and practice, children take another form of the test. When children achieve the mastery criterion, they move to the next skill in the sequence.

Some schools using skills management systems for reading have obtained positive results,[4] but there are worrisome aspects of this approach. A major one is that insufficient attention is given to helping children integrate all of the small subskills into the overall skill of reading. This may be the reason that many children manage to pass the mastery tests without learning to read very well. Another serious problem is that neither research nor conventional wisdom furnishes an agreed-upon division of reading into a sequence of subskills. In short, the Commission believes that skills management systems rest on doubtful assumptions about the process of learning to read. Learning to read appears to involve close knitting of reading skills that complement and support one another, rather than learning one skill, adding a second, then a third, and so on.

Learning to read appears to involve close knitting of reading skills that complement and support one another, rather than learning one skill, adding a second, then a third, and so on.

How Well do Tests Assess Reading?

Standardized tests of reading comprehension manifestly do not measure everything required to understand and appreciate a novel, learn from a science textbook, or find items in a catalogue. A standardized test cannot assess facility in, say, plot analysis because the little passages contrived for standardized tests do not have plots that are sufficiently elaborated to test this facility. The strength of a standardized test is not that it can provide a deep assessment of reading proficiency, but rather that it can provide a fairly reliable, partial assessment cheaply and quickly.

Performance on standardized tests of reading comprehension depends not only on a child's reading ability but also on the child's prior knowledge of the topics addressed in the test passages. When children encounter unfamiliar topics in test passages, they may perform poorly on questions about those passages.[5] They may be able to identify all of the words but may not have enough background knowledge to make the inferences necessary to understand the passage. For example, a rural child trying to read a passage about apartment life in a big city or a child who knows nothing about tennis trying to read a passage about a famous tennis player would be expected to encounter difficulties. Test publishers try to get around this problem by using many short passages about a variety of different topics. Children with extensive knowledge do well on these tests; children with limited knowledge don't. Some groups of children — for example, those who live in environments different than those assumed to be average — are at a disadvantage. They may be able to understand material about the world that is familiar to them, but they do not have the general knowledge needed to do well on standardized reading comprehension tests.

Performance on standardized tests can be influenced by strategies that are not used in normal reading. For instance, "test wise" students develop strategies that help them decide when they can improve their scores on multiple choice tests by guessing.[6] Using these strategies may make these students appear to be better readers than they are. On the other hand, most tests do not permit skilled readers to use strategies that are important in normal reading. For example, good readers use the structure an author has provided to organize, learn, and, ultimately, remember information. Standardized tests as presently constituted do not allow strategies of this type to come into play and, therefore, give an impoverished picture of reading competence.

A more valid assessment of basic reading proficiency than that provided by standardized tests could be obtained by ascertaining whether students can and will do the following: Read aloud unfamiliar but grade-appropriate material with acceptable fluency; write satisfactory summaries of unfamiliar selections from grade-appropriate social studies and science textbooks; explain the plots and motivations of the characters in unfamiliar, grade-appropriate fiction; read extensively from books, magazines, and newspapers during leisure time. A simple, practical suggestion is for teachers to tape record the oral reading of each child three times a year and keep the tapes on file for diagnosis and reporting to parents.

Effects of Tests on Instruction

When they are not under special pressure to improve test scores, school personnel treat standardized tests as just one of several sources of information about student performance.[7] Usually, the correlation between reading test scores and a teacher's ratings of reading ability is moderately high. Thus, in most cases test scores confirm what the teacher already knows.

When a student does *less well* on a standardized test than the teacher expects, generally the test score is discounted, on the grounds that the student probably was anxious, distracted for some reason, or not feeling well. The teacher rightly has more confidence in a judgment based on the voluminous daily record of classroom performance than the brief sample of performance allowed on a test. When a student does *better* than expected on a test, teachers report that this serves as a red flag indicating that the teacher may have underestimated the student.[8]

Research suggests that effective schools make frequent use of tests.[9] Just why this is so is not clear. Some explanations for why it may be so stress the diagnostic

Holding a reading teacher accountable for scores on a test of, say, dividing words into syllables is like holding a basketball coach accountable for the percentage of shots players make during the pre-game warm up.

value of test information — better decisions about placing children in reading groups, more appropriate pace of instruction, more precise analysis of the problems of poor readers, and so on. More plausible is an explanation that stresses accountability: Holding teachers accountable for improved test performance mobilizes and focuses their energies, and those of their students, on academic achievement.

However, holding educators accountable for performance on reading tests as they now exist may have pernicious side-effects.[10] What will happen is that teachers will "teach to the test," not in the fraudulent sense of revealing the answers to particular test items, but in the sense of carefully preparing students for the types of tests that they will be expected to pass.

If the schools are to be held accountable for reading test scores, the tests must be broad-gauged measures that reflect the ultimate goals of instruction as closely as possible. Otherwise, the energies of teachers and students may be misdirected. They may concentrate on peripheral skills that are easily tested and readily learned. Holding a reading teacher accountable for scores on a test of, say, dividing words into syllables is like holding a basketball coach accountable for the percentage of shots players make during the pre-game warm up.

Despite their inherent shortcomings, standardized reading comprehension tests are the most broad-gauged measures of reading proficiency now in general use. The other reading subtests in standardized tests provide information that may be of some diagnostic value for classroom decision-making. However, schools should not overemphasize scores on these subtests, because they measure skills of only subsidiary importance. If scores on the reading comprehension subtest are acceptable, the scores on other subtests need very little attention. For the same reason, schools should not emphasize the "total reading score", since this is a composite that mixes in scores on subtests of lesser significance with the reading comprehension score.

The reading "mastery" tests sold by basal reader publishers and other vendors do not attempt a general assessment of reading comprehension. Instead, these tests cover a large number of subsidiary skills and concepts that are thought to contribute to the development of reading. The results from these tests are supposed to be used to inform classroom-level decisions. In the judgment of the Commission, it is likely that overemphasis on performance on skill mastery tests unbalances a reading program, leading attention away from the integrated act of reading. Probably, increased use of skill mastery tests is one explanation for the extraordinary amount of time devoted to workbook and skill sheet exercises in American classrooms, since these exercises provide direct practice of the skills required to pass the tests.

In conclusion:

- **More comprehensive assessments of reading and writing are needed.** Standardized tests do not provide a deep assessment of reading comprehension and should be supplemented with observations of reading fluency, critical analysis of lengthy reading selections and measures of the amount of independent reading and writing done by children.

- **Tests need to reflect the ultimate goals of reading instruction.** If schools are to be held accountable for test scores, the test scores must be broad-gauged measures which reflect the goals of reading instruction as closely as possible.

- **The proper attitude toward standardized tests is one of balance.** Tests yield information that is of some value, but its significance should not be exaggerated out of proportion.

It is likely that overemphasis on performance on skill mastery tests unbalances a reading program, leading attention away from the integrated act of reading.

Teaching is a complex and demanding profession, more complex than medicine according to one scholar who has studied both professions. Thus, career-long opportunities for growth, renewal, and access to new information are essential.

Teacher Education and Professional Development

A complete picture of learning to read in American schools requires an understanding of those who become reading teachers, the training they receive to enter the profession and to keep abreast of new developments, and the conditions in schools that facilitate or inhibit their work. These matters are discussed in this chapter.

Those Who Become Teachers

Research evidence supports the common sense conclusion that intellectually talented people make the most effective teachers.[1] What may go beyond common sense is the fact that intellectual ability is as important for elementary school teachers as for high school teachers.

Thus, it is an alarming fact that throughout the last decade there has been a decline in the numbers of intellectually talented people entering the teaching profession. College students who choose education as a major have lower average scores on a number of indices of ability than students who select other majors. Among students who begin an education program, those who complete the program have less ability than those who switch to other programs. Among college graduates who get teaching certificates, those who seek teaching jobs are less talented than those who do not. Most alarming

103

of all, among people who take jobs as teachers, those who remain in teaching after five years are less able than those who leave to enter other fields.[2]

Several factors explain the waning attractiveness of the teaching profession: Because of the falling birth rate during the late 60's and the 70's there have been fewer children in school and fewer teaching jobs. In response, the enrollment in teacher education programs has declined. The sharpest decline is among students with the highest ability because they can most easily pursue other career options. For the same reason, the greatest curtailment in teacher education programs is at select colleges and universities. A few great research universities have eliminated undergraduate teacher education altogether, because of lack of student demand and the suspicion that education as a discipline does not meet the standards of the arts and sciences and the prestige professions.

Teachers' salaries are low. In 1984, the average starting salary for a teacher fresh from college was about $14,000, the average starting salary for a person with a bachelor's degree in other fields was about $19,000, and persons with bachelor's degrees in high-demand engineering specialties averaged $25,000 or more.[3] Worse still, teachers' salaries are "front loaded," that is, they are higher at the beginning relative to earnings in other careers; the economic disadvantage of the teacher becomes greater and greater as the years go by.

Poor working conditions contribute to making teaching an unattractive profession for many of the brightest and the best. Teachers generally have less leeway for personal initiative and decision-making than members of other professions. Depending upon the school, they are expected to adhere to policies decreed by administrative superiors, which they have had little or no voice in formulating.[4]

There is no "career ladder" in teaching; the novice has the same job description as the 30-year veteran. People advance in education by moving out of the elementary or secondary school classroom into administration or college teaching.[5]

> It is an alarming fact that throughout the last decade there has been a decline in the numbers of intellectually talented people entering the teaching profession.

Teaching can be a lonely profession. Teachers are isolated every day in classrooms with children, with little opportunity for the stimulation afforded by advice or criticism from colleagues. Indeed, they have very little adult contact of any kind during school hours.[6]

And, it must be acknowledged that the current reform movement has oppressed the spirit of teachers and would-be teachers. The public has been encouraged to hold unrealistic expectations for teachers. When these expectations cannot be met, teachers are faced with anger and contempt. In an essay on *The Lives of Teachers*, one scholar has written,

> Our adult recollections of teachers exaggerate the extremes. We yearn for and idealize the special teacher who changed our life and gave it purpose, and we denigrate the memory of poor teachers who wasted our time and damaged our spirits. The variations, the subtleties, the strengths, and the limitations of the real alive teachers are forgotten over time as the caricatures become fixed . . . Caught between lofty, idealized visions of their work and their low professional status, perceptions of teachers reflect a severe case of cultural ambivalence and uncertainty.[7]

The sharpest decline is among students with the highest ability because they can most easily pursue other career options.

In conclusion, improving reading instruction in the United States is not possible without good teachers. Admissions standards for teacher education programs should be raised. Teacher certification requirements should be stiffened. Beyond these easy steps, better salaries and working conditions are required to recruit and hold good teachers.

The time to act is now. A teacher shortage in the late 1980s looms because school enrollments have stabilized and the supply of new teachers is decreasing. Unless change gets underway now, there will be inevitable pressure to allow less able, less qualified persons to teach.

Education of Future Teachers

Elementary school teachers are generalists. In addition to reading, they have to teach writing, arithmetic, natural science, life science, health, geography, history, and may be expected to teach arts and crafts, music, and physical education. The temptation will be for teachers-in-training to take a smattering of everything and end up not knowing anything in depth. It seems desirable, therefore, for elementary education majors to take a strong academic minor in addition to getting some preparation in each field that they will teach. A logical choice for the academic minor is in the language and communications area, considering the fundamental role that elementary school teachers have in promoting literacy, but perhaps there is room for individual variation in the choice of minor.

About a third of the academic program of an undergraduate majoring in elementary education is devoted to education courses.[8] This amounts to about one and a half years of full-time academic work. Included are foundation courses in the history and philosophy of education, child development, educational psychology, pedagogy courses in methods of teaching reading, methods of teaching arithmetic, and so on, clinical courses that involve observing in classrooms and working with problem children, and apprentice teaching.

Future elementary teachers receive only a basic introduction to reading. Though there is variation depending upon the state and the college or university, the typical undergraduate program includes one course in the teaching of reading and a related course in the teaching of language arts. The reading course may comprise as little as one tenth of the future teacher's academic program during one year of college. Only fleeting treatment can be given to such topics as children's literature, which is basic to getting children involved in extensive reading, or the phonology of English, which provides the foundation for the teaching of phonics. There is not much time for a thorough treatment of reading because the curriculum is crowded. Again, the elementary school teacher is a generalist and future elementary teachers must receive some preparation in many fields.

Education courses provide the most systematic op-

Future elementary teachers receive only a basic introduction to reading. The reading course may comprise as little as one tenth of the future teacher's academic program during one year of college. Only fleeting treatment can be given to such topics as children's literature, or the phonology of English.

portunity for future teachers to acquire the knowledge possessed by the education profession. Critics have doubted that this knowledge amounts to much.[9] Whether the critics are right or wrong is difficult to judge impartially, since evaluating the stock of knowledge possessed by education in comparison, say, to law, medicine, architecture, business administration, or social work is a subjective matter. No doubt people's opinions are influenced by the status of the profession. In any case, however it may compare to the knowledge base of other professions, the stock of trustworthy knowledge in education has increased considerably over the last two decades. Schools with personnel that possess this knowledge, and make use of it, are generally more effective.

Teachers sometimes regard foundation courses in education as too theoretical, not relevant to the practical realities of the classroom. At the same time, courses that are supposed to impart practical know-how are sometimes judged to be simplistic. One reason for these evaluations may be traced to a division in university education faculties between research scholars and teacher educators. Faculty actively involved in research, who typically teach foundation courses, may have received their advanced training in a field outside of education, such as psychology. Often, they have little contact with classroom instruction. Thus, it is not surprising that the courses they teach may be regarded as too theoretical.

On the other hand, there is not a strong tradition of active scholarship among the faculty most directly involved in teacher education. Sometimes they do not keep abreast of the best thinking and research in their fields. This may help to explain why some teaching methods courses are seen as offering a bag of workaday tricks with little intellectual substance. Research-oriented faculty and practice-oriented faculty lead a fitful coexistence in departments of education, especially at major universities. Healing the schism between them is an internal reform that would contribute to the improvement of quality in teacher education programs.[10]

The one aspect of teacher education that is universally

107

endorsed is student teaching. Teachers usually rate it as the most valuable part of their preparation. Studies of student teaching suggest that its value should not be taken for granted, however. One authority has concluded:

> While it may give future teachers a taste of reality, student teaching can also foster bad habits and narrow vision. What helps to solve an immediate problem may not be good teaching. A deceptive sense of success, equated with keeping order and discipline, is liable to close off avenues for further learning.[11]

Teaching skills can be sharpened when student teachers receive frequent and detailed feedback about their teaching. The process is helped when the lessons are videotaped so that features can be analyzed and reanalyzed, strengths and weaknesses pinpointed, and progress charted from one lesson to the next.[12] Probably most future teachers do not receive such intensive training. One reason they do not is that it is expensive. Teacher education has always been funded at a much lower rate per student than education in other professions, a policy that will have to change if substantial improvements are expected.

In summary, prospective elementary school teachers should have more extensive preparation in reading, and perhaps in other fields as well. They require stronger training in the practical aspects of teaching. This cannot be accomplished in four years along with a satisfactory base in the arts and sciences. The conclusion seems inescapable that teacher education programs should be expanded to five years. This is already the policy in some states.

An economic reality will have to be confronted if teacher education programs are to be lengthened to five years. Students in most fields can look forward to a handsome return, in the form of higher future earnings, on the investment they make in a college education. In contrast, there is actually a negative return on the investment in four years of college for students who enter teaching.[13] It would be unrealistic to expect large

There is actually a negative return on the investment in four years of college for students who enter teaching. It would be unrealistic to expect large numbers of able students to make a further economic sacrifice in order to complete a fifth year of teacher training, and it would be unfair of society to expect them to do so.

numbers of able students to make a further economic sacrifice in order to complete a fifth year of teacher training, and it would be unfair of society to expect them to do so. Thus, to be workable, the move to five year teacher education programs should be accompanied by increased scholarship aid, more loans with forgiveness provisions, and, especially, increases in teachers' salaries.

Continuing Professional Development

The first year or two of teaching are extremely difficult for many newcomers to the profession. Beginning teachers often are overwhelmed by having the complete responsibility for a class, anxious about maintaining discipline, and concerned about their effectiveness. Supervisors' appraisals confirm that many new teachers do an unsteady job.

One reason that novice teachers have a difficult time is that they are poorly trained. Another reason is that teacher training institutions do a slack job of evaluation. Too many people of marginal competence are passed through and have to be screened out during their first year on the job. Still, even if training and evaluation were better, probably many people who would eventually become fine teachers find the first couple of years stressful.

Ever since the Conant Report in 1963, there have been calls for programs to assist novice teachers.[14] Nonetheless, most receive little help beyond that which is available to any teacher.[15] This is too bad since good people are lost to the field because of early but correctable failures.

Furthermore, it cannot be assumed that the approaches ingrained during a struggle to survive are necessarily — or even usually — the best teaching practices. Teachers' future professional growth can be limited by a reluctance to give up the practices that helped them get through the first difficult years. A National Institute of Education report concluded that,

> The conditions under which a person carries out the first year of teaching have a strong influence on the level of effectiveness which that teacher is

able to achieve and sustain over the years; on the attitudes which govern teacher behavior over even a forty year career; and indeed, on the decision whether or not to continue in the teaching profession.[16]

Schools that attempt to ease the transition into teaching by appointing experienced teachers to help novices, reducing the teaching load of novices, or engaging consultants to lead continuing seminars for novices have reported favorable results.[17]

Teaching is a complex and demanding profession, more complex than medicine according to one scholar who has studied both professions.[18] Thus, career-long opportunities for growth, renewal, and access to new information are essential. Almost all teachers take additional university courses sometime during their careers. Indeed, about 50% of the experienced teachers in the country have earned masters' degrees. Almost all teachers subscribe to professional magazines. Most teachers attend at least one professional conference or workshop a year.

Schools try to support professional development in several ways. Paid days of leave may be granted to attend professional meetings. Salary increments may be offered for completing university courses. Schools themselves sponsor an average of three workshops a year for teachers.

Doubts can be raised about traditional approaches to stimulating professional development. A salary increment for university course work is no longer a very effective inducement, because most teachers today are veterans and the typical veteran teacher has completed all of the courses for which the school is willing to pay. Income tax deductions are not a strong inducement for teachers since they are in low tax brackets.

Workshops for teachers have characteristic shortcomings. One is that time tends to be filled with discussion of issues, such as detecting child abuse, that can be important in their own right, but which take time away from the central issues of what to teach and how to teach.

Doubts can be raised about traditional approaches to stimulating professional development.

Specialists in the continuing professional development of teachers believe that brief workshops introducing new ideas about teaching seldom lead to enduring changes in classroom practice. Better results are seen when a consultant works with teachers on a number of occasions over a period of time and visits their classrooms in order to assist them in making agreed-upon changes.[19]

Studies of especially effective schools suggest that programs of professional development are most successful when several teachers from the same school, perhaps grade-level teams or maybe the entire faculty, are involved, because they can make a shared commitment to introduce certain changes and can offer one another advice and support. Similarly, changes in practice appear to be more far-reaching and long-lived when the principal, or other responsible administrator, is an active participant, because an innovation is then more likely to have his or her knowledgeable support.[20]

When improvements are needed that are not complicated, but merely require application of easy-to-understand teaching principles that teachers ought to know but don't always practice, something as simple as giving them a brief guide listing the principles has proved successful in boosting children's achievement in reading and arithmetic.[21] This technique works better, however, when teachers have the opportunity to meet and discuss the principles and when someone visits their classes occasionally, so that they are reminded to continue to use the principles.[22]

To summarize, every school should make special provisions to ease the induction of newcomers into the teaching profession. At the same time, renewed attention should be given to the professional growth of veteran teachers so that they can continue to approach teaching with zest and can have access to new knowledge that will allow them to improve their teaching. The nation's corp of teachers is older, more stable, and more experienced than any time in history. It is a simple matter of arithmetic that reforms in education depend upon sustaining the vigor and the skill of veteran teachers.

The Ethos of Effective Schools

Every school has a distinct personality, or "ethos," that reflects the community it serves, the students who attend, the building it inhabits, the staff who labor in it, its history and traditions, and its values and policies.[23] The picture of influences on learning to read would be incomplete if it stopped with the approach to phonics taken by the first-grade teachers, or the style of questioning of the third-grade teachers, or the content of lessons on study skills presented by the fifth-grade teachers. A school is more than a collection of individual classrooms. For illustration of this point, consider that an individual teacher is likely to have trouble maintaining discipline in his or her classroom if bedlam reigns in the halls, bathrooms, and adjoining classrooms.

From studies of schools that produce achievement beyond that which would be expected considering the composition of the students, a picture of effective schools has emerged. Studies of this type are difficult to do and taken one at a time each has flaws and limitations.[24] Nevertheless, one can have a fair degree of confidence in the validity of features that have appeared consistently, particularly since several of the features seem to be generally characteristic of successful human organizations ranging from winning sports teams to productive manufacturing plants.

Schools that are especially effective in teaching children to read are characterized by vigorous instructional leadership.[25] The leader is usually the principal, though it may be another administrator such as the reading supervisor, or leadership may come from a group of faculty members. Undoubtedly, there is a range of leadership styles that can be effective depending upon the circumstances. In education, though, the leader who achieves good results by directive and administrative fiat, without consultation with others, is probably the exception. It is difficult to produce excellence by command when what goes on behind closed classroom doors is not easily monitored or controlled.

Instructional leadership in reading entails a considerable amount of specialized knowledge and experience. Yet there are still states that certify people as elementary

> **Every school has a distinct personality, or "ethos," that reflects the community it serves, the students who attend, the building it inhabits, the staff who labor in it, its history and traditions, and its values and policies.**

school principals who have neither training nor experience as elementary teachers, who have never taught a child to read, and who have never coped with a child having trouble learning to read. When the principal lacks adequate knowledge of reading, other members of the staff must furnish instructional leadership.

Schools that are especially effective in teaching reading have high but realistic expectations about the progress that students will make in reading. One function the leader serves in these schools is to keep attention focused on reading and to keep expectations high. In these schools, academic excellence is honored in school ceremonies along with the skill of the chorus or band and the conquests of the athletic teams. In these schools, children's progress in reading is closely monitored by formal and informal means; the staff is persistent in seeking remedies for children whose progress is unsatisfactory.

Schools that are especially effective in teaching reading are characterized by school pride, collegiality, and a sense of community. Teachers collaborate in planning in these schools. This means that there is more likely to be agreement on goals and more likely to be understanding of and commitment to policies for achieving these goals. In particular, the reading program tends to be more stable with a clearer articulation of what will be taught in the various grades and, thus, there are neither gaps nor needless repetition. There is more coordination in handling difficult-to-teach and difficult-to-manage children. Programs for professional development tend to be conducted on a schoolwide basis with participation from teachers in deciding what form the programs will take. There is less staff turnover and staff absenteeism than in comparable but less effective schools.

Schools that are especially effective in teaching reading are characterized by order and discipline. That this is so is only common sense. In addition to reducing distractions and making schools more safe and pleasant, reasonable rules, consistently enforced, can contribute to school pride. A similar contribution may be made by

Instructional leadership in reading entails a considerable amount of specialized knowledge and experience. Yet there are still states that certify people as elementary school principals who have neither training nor experience as elementary teachers, who have never taught a child to read, and who have never coped with a child having trouble learning to read.

insisting that a school is kept clean, neat, and in good repair.

Schools that are especially effective in teaching reading maximize the amount of uninterrupted time available for learning. This is one reason why discipline and order are important. Smaller but significant contributions to time for learning are made by restricting announcements over the public address system, minimizing the clerical chores and other noninstructional demands on teachers' time, and careful scheduling of special events, rehearsals, health examinations, classroom visitors, and remedial teachers who pull children out of class.

It is difficult for a teacher here and there with high aspirations and well-honed skills to achieve excellence if the school lacks leadership or the ethos of the school is indifferent to academic learning, order and discipline, and collegiality.

In conclusion:

- **Improving reading instruction in the United States is not possible without good teachers.** Admission standards for teacher education programs and teacher certification requirements should be raised. Beyond these easy steps, better salaries and working conditions are required to recruit and hold good teachers.

- **Teacher education programs need improvement.** The schism between research oriented and practice oriented faculty needs to be bridged. Elementary teachers need more extensive preparation in reading and stronger training in the practical aspects of teaching.

- **Schools should make special provisions to ease the induction of newcomers into the teaching profession.** At the same time, attention needs to be given to the professional growth of veteran teachers so they will continue to approach teaching with zest and have access to new knowledge.

- **The ethos of the school should promote literacy.** Vigorous instructional leadership, high expectations for children, a high priority for literacy, order and discipline, uninterrupted learning time, and a sense of community characterize effective schools.

> It is difficult for a teacher here and there with high aspirations and well-honed skills to achieve excellence if the school lacks leadership or the ethos of the school is indifferent to academic learning, order and discipline, and collegiality.

America will become a nation of readers when verified practices of the best teachers in the best schools can be introduced throughout the country.

Becoming a Nation of Readers: Recommendations

The more elements of good parenting, good teaching, and good schooling that children experience, the greater the likelihood that they will achieve their potential as readers. The following recommendations encapsulate the information presented in this report about the conditions likely to produce citizens who read with high levels of skill and do so frequently with evident satisfaction.

Parents should read to preschool children and informally teach them about reading and writing. Reading to children, discussing stories and experiences with them, and — with a light touch — helping them learn letters and words are practices that are consistently associated with eventual success in reading.

Parents should support school-aged children's continued growth as readers. Parents of children who become successful readers monitor their children's progress in school, become involved in school programs, support homework, buy their children books or take them to libraries, encourage reading as a free time activity, and place reasonable limits on such activities as TV viewing.

Preschool and kindergarten reading readiness programs should focus on reading, writing, and oral language. Knowledge of letters and their sounds, words, stories, and question asking and answering are related to learning to read, but there is little evidence that such activities as coloring, cutting with a scissors, or discriminating shapes (except the shapes of letters) promote reading development.

Teachers should maintain classrooms that are both stimulating and disciplined. Effective teachers of reading create a literate classroom environment. They allocate an adequate amount of time to reading and writing, sustain children's attention, maintain a brisk pace, and keep rates of success high.

Teachers of beginning reading should present well-designed phonics instruction. Though most children today are taught phonics, often this instruction is poorly conceived. Phonics is more likely to be useful when children hear the sounds associated with most letters both in isolation and in words, and when they are taught to blend together the sounds of letters to identify words. In addition, encouraging children to think of other words they know with similar spellings, when they encounter words they cannot readily identify, may help them develop the adult strategy of decoding unknown words by analogy with ones that are known. Phonics instruction should be kept simple and it should be completed by the end of the second grade for most children.

Reading primers should be interesting, comprehensible, and give children opportunities to apply phonics. There should be a close interplay between phonics instruction and reading words in meaningful selections. But most primers contain too few words that can be identified using the phonics that has already been taught. After the very earliest selections, primers should tell complete, interesting stories.

Teachers should devote more time to comprehension instruction. Teacher-led instruction in reading strategies and other aspects of comprehension promotes reading achievement, but there is very little direct comprehension instruction in most American classrooms.

Children should spend less time completing workbooks and skill sheets. Workbook and skill sheet activities consume a large proportion of the time allocated to reading instruction in most American classrooms, despite the fact that there is little evidence that these activities are related to reading achievement. Workbook and skill sheet activities should be pared to the minimum that actually provide worthwhile practice in aspects of reading.

Children should spend more time in independent reading. Independent reading, whether in school or out of school, is associated with gains in reading achievement. By the time they are in the third or fourth grade, children should read independently a minimum of two hours per week. Children's reading should include classic and modern works of fiction and nonfiction that represent the core of our cultural heritage.

Children should spend more time writing. Opportunities to write more than a sentence or two are infrequent in most American elementary school classrooms. As well as being valuable in its own right, writing promotes ability in reading.

Textbooks should contain adequate explanations of important concepts. Textbooks in science, social studies, and other areas should be clearly written, well-organized, and contain important information and concepts. Too many of the textbooks used in American classrooms do not meet these standards.

Schools should cultivate an ethos that supports reading. Schools that are effective in teaching reading are characterized by vigorous leadership, high expectations, an emphasis on academic learning, order and discipline, uninterrupted time for learning, and staffs that work together.

Schools should maintain well-stocked and managed libraries. Access to interesting and informative books is one of the keys to a successful reading program. As important as an adequate collection of books is a librarian who encourages wide reading and helps match books to children.

119

Schools should introduce more comprehensive assessments of reading and writing. Standardized tests should be supplemented with assessments of reading fluency, ability to summarize and critically evaluate lengthy selections, amount of independent reading, and amount and quality of writing.

Schools should attract and hold more able teachers. The number of able people who choose teaching as a profession has declined in recent years. Reversing this trend requires higher admissions standards for teacher education programs, stronger standards for teacher certification, improved working conditions, and higher teachers' salaries.

Teacher education programs should be lengthened and improved in quality. Prospective elementary teachers do not acquire an adequate base in either the liberal arts and sciences or in pedagogy. They get only a fleeting introduction to the knowledge required for teaching reading. Teacher education programs should be extended to five years and the quality and rigor of the instruction should be increased.

Schools should provide for the continuing professional development of teachers. Schools should have programs to ease the transition of novice teachers into the profession and programs to keep veteran teachers abreast of advancing knowledge.

America will become a nation of readers when verified practices of the best teachers in the best schools can be introduced throughout the country.

Afterword

It is a privilege to be invited to write this afterword — as a member of the Commission on Reading, the National Academy of Education, and as co-editor, with John B. Carroll, of the earlier Academy report on reading, *Toward a Literate Society* (McGraw-Hill, 1975).

> The [earlier] Committee on Reading was appointed by the Executive Council of the National Academy of Education in response to a letter, dated December 5, 1969, from the then Assistant Secretary (HEW) for Education and United States Commissioner of Education James E. Allen, Jr., to Dr. Lawrence A. Cremin, then President of the Academy, asking for basic guidance in the conduct of the Right-to-Read program, which Commissioner Allen had first announced in an address to the National Association of State Boards of Education on September 23, 1969. (p. xi)

The mission of the Right-to-Read program was to achieve universal literacy and to make real the belief that reading is a right, not a privilege, for all Americans — with special emphasis on children and adults whose reading is below par. The essential task for the Committee on Reading was to seek out the existing scientific knowledge and the knowledge still needed to achieve universal literacy.

The report and the position papers of *Toward a Literate Society* provided a comprehensive view of the scientific knowledge on child and adult literacy, with an emphasis on overcoming the problems of those with the greatest need through efforts of schools, industry, technology, and government.

The present Commission on Reading, similarly appointed by the president of the National Academy, now Robert Glaser, had a more specific focus — to bring to bear the great mass of research and theory on "beginning reading and the comprehension of language" for the improvement of reading in all children. Overall, a shorter work (without individually authored position papers), it is nevertheless a remarkable synthesis of the vast recent research on reading, which too often seems to have conflicting and controversial findings. The Commission members were appointed, in fact, to represent some of these differing viewpoints in reading, and our long and lively discussions would, in themselves, make a fascinating story.

But we did come to a consensus on most issues, and in a relatively short time. I will, therefore, limit my afterword to one issue — that of persons who have serious reading difficulties — which continues to be of great concern and stress for many children, young people, adults, their families, and those who are responsible for helping them. Millions of children and adults have special problems in learning to read and tend to remain behind in reading and related academic subjects unless they are given extra help. This group includes children from low income families, ethnic minorities, non-English or recent speakers of English, and those with specific reading and learning disabilities. This group also includes illiterates and adults who are only functionally literate. Taken together, various estimates indicate that they may now make up about a third or more of the population — some tens of millions of people. Many of their problems can, of course, be significantly lessened in the coming generations if the knowledge contained in this report is used wisely and well. We know from health care, however, that although prevention is essential, treatment is nonetheless needed for those already having problems.

Let us take one of these special groups as an example — those with severe reading and learning disabilities, often referred to as having dyslexia. There is general agreement among researchers that from 10 to 15 percent of the population is so handicapped. Their reading achievement lags significantly behind their mental abilities and language comprehension. Although improved instruction makes it easier for them to learn to read, their difficulties often persist and take different forms as they progress. They learn, and they do best when they receive proper diagnosis and remediation. And the earlier they are given these, the better.[1]

Thus, it would seem that in order to effect a significant improvement in reading for children and adults with reading/learning disability, we will need to plan for more care, more funds, and more professional help both to prevent and treat their difficulties.

The same can be said for others who experience difficulty. The Commission's delineation of the reading process and its recommendations for practice will be useful for them as well. But they will usually need additional help if they are to reach reading abilities on a par with their cognitive and language abilities. Thus, in a recent study on the course of development of reading, writing, and language among middle grade children from low income families, we found that while in the first three grades their achievement fell within the normal range for their grades, beginning with about grade 4, many began to fall behind. However, those who were in classes where teachers stressed the development of comprehension and word meanings, where their textbooks were on a challenging level, and where they were exposed to a wide range of library books, did not decelerate in reading. Indeed, they continued to gain.[2]

A further word is needed, also, with regard to improving adult literacy. Traditionally, teachers of adults have tended to see their task as essentially different from that of teaching reading to children and young people. While one must recognize differences in maturity, in experience, and in goals, adult educators and those who teach adults to read can find much in this report to help them. Especially relevant is the progression of reading skills, abilities, and tasks presented in the report — from its beginnings to higher levels of reading. After adjustments are made in materials and in emphasis, this progression may be useful for teaching adults as well.[3]

The underlying causes of the reading difficulties of individuals are not always easy to detect. But research, as well as clinical practice over the past decades, indicate that what often appears as lack of motivation, listlessness, and hopelessness may stem from other, more fundamental causes. And, the research and practice also indicate that the best treatment is excellent instruction, which in turn seems to heighten interest and hope as well as improve reading skills and uses of reading. Thus concern for individual needs, as well as improved instruction and stimulation in schools and at home, will be needed if we are to truly become a nation of readers.

Jeanne Chall
Professor and Director
Reading Laboratory
Graduate School of Education
Harvard University

Appendices

References and Notes

Introduction

1. Psacharopoulos, G. (1981). Returns to education: An updated international comparison. *Comparative Education, 17,* 321-341.

2. National Commission on Excellence in Education. (1983). *A nation at risk: The imperative for educational reform.* Washington, DC: U.S. Department of Education.

3. There is reason to believe that instructional materials and quality of teaching in the early grades can significantly influence higher level achievement at high school and college. See Chall, J. S. (1983). Literacy: Trends and explanations. *Educational Researcher, 12,* 3-8.

4. See Farr, R., & Fay, L. (1982). Reading trend data in the United States: A mandate for caveats and caution. In G. R. Austin & H. Garber (Eds.), *The rise and fall of national test scores* (pp. 83-141). New York: Academic Press.

5. Gates, A. I. (1961). *Attainment in elementary schools: 1957 and 1937.* New York: Bureau of Publications, Columbia Teachers College.

6. National Assessment of Educational Progress. (1981). *Three national assessments of reading:Changes in performance, 1970-1980* (Report 11-R-01). Denver, CO: Education Commission of the States.

7. Chall (1983) op. cit.

   Eckland, B. K. (1982). College entrance examination trends. In G. R. Austin & H. Garber (Eds.), *The rise and fall of national test scores* (pp. 9-34). New York: Academic Press.

   Farr & Fay (1982) op. cit.

   Harnischfeger, A., & Wiley, D. E. (1975). *Achievement test scores decline: Do we need to worry?* Chicago, IL: CEMREL.

   Some NAEP data also tend to support the decline in more advanced reading skill. Between the 1970-71 and 1979-80 NAEP evaluations, 17-year-olds showed slight losses in inferential comprehension.

8. See Eckland (1982) op. cit.

9. Thorndike, R. L. (1973). *Reading comprehension education in fifteen countries: An empirical study.* New York: Wiley.

10. Stevenson, H. W. (1984). Making the grade: School achievement in Japan, Taiwan, and

the United States. *Annual Report of the Center for Advanced Study in the Behavioral Sciences* (pp. 41-51). Stanford, CA.

11. Historical research shows a steady increase in the standards of literacy required to meet changing social needs and conditions. See Resnick, D. P., & Resnick, L. B. (1977). The nature of literacy: An historical exploration. *Harvard Educational Review, 47,* 370-385.

What Is Reading?

1. Adapted from Schallert, D. L. (1982). The significance of knowledge: A synthesis of research related to schema theory. In W. Otto & S. White (Eds.), *Reading expository material* (pp. 13-48). New York: Academic Press, p. 28.

2. Pearson, P. D., & Spiro, R. J. (1980). Toward a theory of reading comprehension instruction. *Topics in Language Disorders, 1,* 71-88.

3. Oral reading errors showing an overreliance on graphophonemic cues are described in:

   Hood, J., & Kendall, J. R. (1975). Qualitative analysis of oral reading errors of reflective and impulsive second graders: Follow-up study. *Journal of Reading Behavior, 7,* 269-281.

   Weber, R. M. (1970). A linguistic analysis of first-grade reading errors. *Reading Research Quarterly, 5,* 427-451.

4. Oral reading errors showing an overreliance on contextual cues are described in Biemiller, A. (1970). The development of the use of graphic and contextual information as children learn to read. *Reading Research Quarterly, 6,* 75-96.

5. Steffensen, M. S., Joag-dev, C., & Anderson, R. C. (1979). A cross-cultural perspective on reading comprehension. *Reading Research Quarterly, 15,* 10-29.

6. Pearson, P. D., Hansen, J., & Gordon, C. (1979). The effect of background knowledge on young children's comprehension of explicit and implicit information. *Journal of Reading Behavior, 11,* 201-209.

7. Owings, R. A., Peterson, G. A., Bransford, J. D., Morris, C. D., & Stein, B. S. (1980). Spontaneous monitoring and regulation of learning: A comparison of successful and less successful fifth graders. *Journal of Educational Psychology, 72,* 250-256.

   Paris, S. G., & Lindauer, B. K. (1976). The role of inference in children's comprehension and memory for sentences. *Cognitive Psychology, 8,* 217-227.

   For implications of children's failure to draw on prior knowledge in the school setting, see:

   Beck, I. L. (1985). Five problems with children's comprehension in the primary grades. In J. Osborn, P. T. Wilson, & R. C. Anderson (Eds.), *Reading education: Foundations for a literate America* (pp. 239-253). Lexington, MA: Lexington Books.

   Wilson, P. T., & Anderson, R. C. (1985). Reading comprehension and school learning. In J. Osborn, P. T. Wilson, & R. C. Anderson (Eds.), *Reading education: Foundations for a literate America* (pp. 319-328). Lexington, MA: Lexington Books.

8. Lesgold, A., Resnick, L. B., & Hammond, K. (1985). Learning to read: A longitudinal study of word skill development in two curricula. In T. G. Waller & G. E. MacKinnon (Eds.), *Reading research: Advances in theory and practice* (Vol. 4, pp. 107-138). New York: Academic Press.

9. Cattell, J. M. (1886). The time it takes to see and name objects. *Mind, 11,* 63-65.

10. Meyer, D. E., & Schvaneveldt, R. W. (1971). Facilitation in recognizing pairs of words: Evidence of a dependence between retrieval operations. *Journal of Experimental Psychology, 90,* 227-234. This study shows facilitation effects with words presented in isolation. There is evidence to suggest that contextual constraints also facilitate processing during reading of connected text. See Zola, D. (1984). Redundancy and word perception during reading. *Perception and Psychophysics, 36,* 277-284.

11. McClelland, J. L., & Rumelhart, D. E. (1981). An interactive activation model of context effects in letter perception: Part 1. An account of basic findings. *Psychological Review, 88,* 375-407.

    Rumelhart, D. E., & McClelland, J. L. (1982). An interactive activation model of context effects in letter perception: Part 2. The contextual enhancement effect and some tests and extensions of the model. *Psychological Review, 89,* 60-94.

12. Gough, P. B. (1972). One second of reading.

In J. F. Kavanagh & I. G. Mattingly (Eds.), *Language by ear and by eye* (pp. 331-358). Cambridge, MA: MIT Press.

Just, M. A., & Carpenter, P. A. (1980). A theory of reading: From eye fixations to comprehension. *Psychological Review, 87,* 329-354.

13. Stanovich, K. E. (1980). Toward an interactive-compensatory model of individual differences in the development of reading fluency. *Reading Research Quarterly, 16,* 32-71.

14. Glushko, R. J. (1979). The organization and activation of orthographic knowledge in reading aloud. *Journal of Experimental Psychology: Human Perception and Performance, 5,* 674-691.

McClelland & Rumelhart (1981) op. cit.

Rumelhart & McClelland (1982) op. cit.

15. Perfetti, C. A., & Lesgold, A. M. (1977). Discourse comprehension and sources of individual differences. In M. A. Just & P. A. Carpenter (Eds.), *Cognitive processes in comprehension* (pp. 141-183). Hillsdale, NJ: Erlbaum.

16. Anderson, R. C., & Kulhavy R. W. (1972). Learning concepts from definitions. *American Educational Research Journal, 9,* 385-390.

Anderson, R. C., Goldberg, S. R., & Hidde, J. L. (1971). Meaningful processing of sentences. *Journal of Educational Psychology, 62,* 395-399.

17. Hoffman, J. V., O'Neal, S. F., Kastler, L. A., Clements, R. O., Segel, K. W., & Nash, M. F. (1984). Guided oral reading and miscue focused verbal feedback in second-grade classrooms. *Reading Research Quarterly, 19,* 367-384.

18. Lesgold, Resnick, & Hammond (1985) op. cit.

19. See Baker, L., & Brown, A. L. (1984). Metacognitive skills and reading. In P. D. Pearson (Ed.), *Handbook of reading research* (pp. 353-394). New York: Longman.

20. Forrest, D. L., & Waller, T. G. (1979, March). *Cognitive and metacognitive aspects of reading.* Paper presented at the biennial meeting of the Society for Research in Child Development, San Francisco, CA.

21. From Grabe, M., & Mann, S. (1984). A technique for the assessment and training of comprehension monitoring skills. *Journal of Reading Behavior, 16,* 131-144, p. 136.

22. Ibid.

23. Myers, M., & Paris, S. G. (1978). Children's metacognitive knowledge about reading. *Journal of Educational Psychology, 70,* 680-690.

24. Paris, S. G., & Myers, M. (1981). Comprehension monitoring, memory, and study strategies of good and poor readers. *Journal of Reading Behavior, 13,* 5-22.

25. Durkin, D. (1982). *A study of poor black children who are successful readers* (Reading Ed. Rep. No. 33). Urbana: University of Illinois, Center for the Study of Reading.

26. See Walberg, H. J., Hare, V. C., & Pulliam, C. A. (1981). Social-psychological perceptions and reading comprehension. In J. T. Guthrie (Ed.), *Comprehension and teaching: Research reviews* (pp. 140-159). Newark, DE: International Reading Association.

27. See Dweck, C. S. (1975). The role of expectations and attributions in the alleviation of learned helplessness. *Journal of Personality and Social Psychology, 31,* 674-685.

28. Weiner, B. (1983). Some thoughts about feelings. In S. G. Paris, G. M. Olson, & H. W. Stevenson (Eds.), *Learning and motivation in the classroom* (pp. 165-178). Hillsdale, NJ: Erlbaum.

29. Hoffman et al. (1984) op. cit.

Rosenshine, B., & Stevens, R. (1984). Classroom instruction in reading. In P. D. Pearson (Ed.), *Handbook of reading research* (pp. 745-798). New York: Longman.

30. Brophy, J. E. (1983). Fostering student learning and motivation in the elementary school classroom. In S. G. Paris, G. M. Olson, & H. W. Stevenson (Eds.), *Learning and motivation in the classroom* (pp. 283-305). Hillsdale, NJ: Erlbaum.

31. See Chall, J. S. (1983). *Stages of reading development.* New York: McGraw-Hill.

Emerging Literacy

1. Heath, S. B. (1983). *Ways with words: Language, life and work in communities and classrooms.* New York: Cambridge University Press.

2. Wilson, P. T., & Anderson, R. C. (1985). Reading comprehension and school learning. In J. Osborn, P. T. Wilson, & R. C. Anderson (Eds.), *Reading education: Foundations for a literate America* (pp. 319-328). Lexington, MA: Lexington Books.

3. Olson, D. R. (1984). "See! Jumping!" Some

oral language antecedents of literacy. In H. Goelman, A. Oberg & F. Smith (Eds.), *Awakening to literacy* (pp. 185-192). Exeter, NH: Heinemann.

Snow, C. E., & Ferguson, C. A. (Eds.). (1977). *Talking to children: Language input and acquisition.* Cambridge, MA: Cambridge University Press.

4. Wells, G. (1981). *Learning through interaction: The study of language development.* New York: Cambridge University Press.

Wells, G. (1983). Language and learning in the early years. *Early Child Development and Care, 11,* 69-77.

Similarly, the experience of listening to, and talking about, stories provides children with the opportunity to learn the importance of attending to events removed from the immediate here and now. See Heath, S. B. (1982). What no bedtime story means: Narrative skills at home and school. *Language in Society, 11,* 49-76.

5. Wells, G. (1981). Some antecedents of early educational attainment. *British Journal of Sociology of Education, 2,* 181-200.

6. Chomsky, C. (1972). Stages in language development and reading exposure. *Harvard Educational Review, 42,* 1-33.

Durkin, D. (1966). *Children who read early: Two longitudinal studies.* New York: Teachers College Press.

McCormick, S. (1977). Should you read aloud to your children? *Language Arts, 54,* 139-143.

7. Heath (1982) op. cit.

8. Heath (1982) op. cit.

9. Chomsky, C. (1976). After decoding: What? *Language Arts, 53,* 288-296; 314.

Samuels, S. J. (1985). Automaticity and repeated reading. In J. Osborn, P. T. Wilson, & R. C. Anderson (Eds.), *Reading education: Foundations for a literate America* (pp. 215-230). Lexington, MA: Lexington Books.

10. Durkin (1966) op. cit.

11. Research with very young children on invented spelling suggests that children's early experiences with "writing" may promote the development of letter-sound knowledge. E.g.:

Chomsky, C. (1971). Write first, read later. *Childhood Education, 47,* 296-299.

Chomsky, C. (1979). Approaching reading through invented spelling. In L. B. Resnick & P. A. Weaver (Eds.), *Theory and practice of early reading* (Vol. 2, pp. 43-65). Hillsdale, NJ: Erlbaum.

12. See Dunn, N. E. (1981). Children's achievement at school-entry age as a function of mothers' and fathers' teaching sets. *Elementary School Journal, 81,* 245-253.

13. Brzeinski, J. E. (1964). Beginning reading in Denver. *The Reading Teacher, 18,* 16-21. Also see Taylor, D. (1983). *Family literacy: Young children learning to read and write.* Exeter, NH: Heinemann.

14. Dunn (1981) op. cit. A similar finding is reported by Hess, R. D., Holloway, S., Price, G. G., & Dickson, W. (1979, November). *Family environments and acquisition of reading skills: Toward a more precise analysis.* Paper presented at the Conference on the Family as a Learning Environment, Educational Testing Service, Princeton, NJ.

15. See:

Ball, S., & Bogatz, G. A. (1970). *The first year of "Sesame Street": An evaluation.* Princeton, NJ: Educational Testing Service.

Bogatz, G. A., & Ball, S. (1971). *The second year of "Sesame Street": A continuing evaluation.* Princeton, NJ.: Educational Testing Service.

Minton, J. H. (1972). *The impact of "Sesame Street" on reading readiness of kindergarten children.* Unpublished doctoral dissertation, Fordham University.

16. Entwistle, D., & Hayduk, L. (1978). *Too great expectations: The academic outlook of young children.* Baltimore, MD: Johns Hopkins University Press.

17. Stevenson, H. W. (1984). Making the grade: School achievement in Japan, Taiwan, and the United States. *Annual Report of the Center for Advanced Study in the Behavioral Sciences* (pp. 41-51). Stanford, CA.

18. Walberg, H. J., & Tsai, S. (1984). Reading achievement and diminishing returns to time. *Journal of Educational Psychology, 76,* 442-451.

19. See Becker, H. J., & Epstein, J. L. (1982). Parent involvement: A survey of teacher practice. *Elementary School Journal, 83,* 85-102.

20. Fielding, L. G., Wilson, P. T., & Anderson, R. C. (in press). A new focus on free reading:

The role of trade books in reading instruction. In T. Raphael & R. Reynolds (Eds.), *Contexts of literacy*. New York: Longman.

21. Ibid.

22. Williams, P. A., Haertel, E. H., Haertel, G. D., & Walberg, H. J. (1982). The impact of leisure-time television on school learning: A research synthesis. *American Educational Research Journal, 19,* 19-50.

23. See Note 15.

24. The term "readiness" was first explicitly applied to reading in 1925. See National Society for the Study of Education. (1925). *Report of the National Committee on Reading.* 24th Year Book of the National Society for the Study of Education. Bloomington, IN: Public School Publishing. Of the large number of papers on reading readiness which appeared during the 1930s, the most influential were:

Dolch, E. W., & Bloomster, M. (1937). Phonic readiness. *Elementary School Journal, 38,* 201-205.

Morphett, M. V., & Washburne, C. (1931). When should children begin to read? *Elementary School Journal, 31,* 496-503.

25. Robinson, H. M. (1972). Perceptual training: Does it result in reading improvement? In R. C. Aukerman (Ed.), *Some persistent questions on beginning reading*. Newark, DE: International Reading Association. There is also evidence, as indicated in this paper, that some of the tasks that children are supposed to master in the name of "reading" are actually harder for many children than reading words.

26. E.g.:

Beck, I. L. (1973). *A longitudinal study of the reading achievement effects of formal reading instruction in the kindergarten: A summative and formative evaluation.* Unpublished doctoral dissertation, University of Pittsburgh.

Bissex, G. (1980). *Gnys at wrk: A child learns to write and read.* Cambridge, MA: Harvard University Press.

Durkin, D. (1974-75). A six year study of children who learned to read in school at the age of four. *Reading Research Quarterly, 10,* 9-61.

Soderbergh, R. (1977). *Reading in early childhood: A linguistic study of a preschool child's gradual acquisition of reading ability.* Washington, DC: Georgetown University Press.

Taylor (1983) op. cit.

27. Becker, W. C., & Engelmann, S. (1978). *Analysis of achievement data on six cohorts of low-income children from 20 school districts in the University of Oregon Direct Instruction Follow Through Model* (Follow Through Project, Tech. Rep. No. 78-1). Eugene, OR: University of Oregon.

Meyer, L. A., Gersten, R. M., & Gutkin, J. (1983). Direct Instruction: A Project Follow Through success story in an inner-city school. *The Elementary School Journal, 84,* 241-252.

28. Darlington, R. B. (1981). The consortium for longitudinal studies. *Educational Evaluation and Policy Analysis, 3,* 37-45.

Lazar, I., Hubbel, V. R., Murray, H., Rosche, M., & Royce, J. (1977). *The persistence of preschool effects.* Washington, DC: Department of Health Education and Welfare.

Schweinhart, L. J., & Weikart, D. P. (1980). *Young children grow up: The effects of the Perry Preschool program on youths through age 15.* Ypsilanti, MI: High Scope Educational Research Foundation.

29. See:

Bagford, J. (1968). Reading readiness scores and success in reading. *The Reading Teacher, 21,* 324-328.

Lohnes, P. R., & Gray, M. M. (1972). Intelligence and the Cooperative Reading Studies. *Reading Research Quarterly, 7,* 466-476.

However, some studies report a weaker relationship between early listening comprehension proficiency and third grade reading achievement. E.g. Muehl, S., & Di Nello, M. C. (1976). Early first-grade skills related to subsequent reading performance: A seven year follow-up study. *Journal of Reading Behavior, 8,* 67-81.

30. Atkin, R., Bray, R., Davison, M., Herzberger, S., Humphreys, L., & Selzer, U. (1977). Cross-lagged panel analysis of sixteen cognitive measures at four grade levels. *Journal for Research in Child Development, 48,* 944-952. A review and an extension of this work appears in Humphreys, L. G., & Davey, T. C. (1983). *Anticipation of gains in general information: A comparison of verbal aptitude, reading comprehension, and listening* (Tech. Rep. No. 282).

Urbana: University of Illinois, Center for the Study of Reading.

31. See Mason, J. M. (1984). Early reading from a developmental perspective. In P. D. Pearson (Ed.), *Handbook of reading research* (pp. 505-543). New York: Longman.

32. Hiebert, E. H., & Sawyer, C. C. (1984, April). *Young children's concurrent abilities in reading and spelling.* Paper presented at the annual meeting of the American Educational Research Association, New Orleans, LA. Similar trends have been reported in Mason, J. M. (1980). When do children begin to read: An exploration of four-year-old children's letter and word reading competencies. *Reading Research Quarterly, 15,* 203-227.

33. Barrett, T. (1965). The relationship between measures of prereading, visual discrimination and first grade reading achievement: A review of the literature. *Reading Research Quarterly, 1,* 51-76.

Bond, G. L., & Dykstra, R. (1967). The co-operative research program in first-grade reading instruction (entire issue). *Reading Research Quarterly, 2(4).*

de Hirsch, K., Jansky, J. J, & Langford, W. D. (1966). *Predicting reading failure: A preliminary study.* New York: Harper & Row.

34. The effects of training in letter-names alone have been reported in:

Muehl, S. (1962). The effects of letter-name knowledge on learning to read a word list in kindergarten children. *Journal of Educational Psychology, 53,* 181-186.

Samuels, S. J. (1972). The effect of letter-name knowledge on learning to read. *American Educational Research Journal, 9,* 65-74.

Silberberg, N. E., Silberberg, M. C., & Iversen, I. A. (1972). The effects of kindergarten instruction in alphabet and numbers on first grade reading. *Journal of Learning Disabilities, 5,* 254-261.

Venezky, R. L. (1975). The curious role of letter names in reading instruction. *Visible Language, 9,* 7-23.

The benefits in training in both letter-names and letter-sounds have been reported in Ohnmacht, D. D. (1969). *The effects of letter-knowledge on achievement in reading in the first grade.* Paper presented at the annual meeting of the American Educational Research Association, Los Angeles, CA. There is also evidence indicating that improved decoding ability is achieved when letter-sound training is combined with other types of training. See Jeffrey, W. E., & Samuels, S. J. (1967). The effect of method of reading training on initial learning and transfer. *Journal of Verbal Learning and Verbal Behavior, 6,* 354-358.

35. Clay, M. M. (1972). *Reading, the patterning of complex behavior.* Auckland, NZ: Heinemann.

Downing, J. (1979, June). *Cognitive clarity and linguistic awareness.* Paper presented at the International Seminar on Linguistic Awareness and Learning to Read, University of Victoria, Victoria, BC.

Ehri, L. (1979). Linguistic insight: Threshold of reading acquisition. In T. G. Waller & G. E. MacKinnon (Eds.), *Reading research: Advances in theory and practice* (Vol. 1, pp. 63-114). New York: Academic Press.

Goodman, K., & Goodman, Y. (1979). Learning to read is natural. In L. B. Resnick & P. A. Weaver (Eds.), *Theory and practice of early reading* (Vol. 1, pp. 137-154). Hillsdale, NJ: Erlbaum.

Harste, J. C., Burke, C. L., & Woodward, V. A. (1982). Children's language and world: Initial encounters with print. In J. Langer & M. Trika Smith-Burke (Eds.), *Reader meets author / Bridging the gap* (pp. 105-131). Newark, DE: International Reading Association.

Mason (1980) op. cit.

36. For thoughtful discussions of children's first learning of words, letters, and sounds, see:

Ehri, L. C., & Wilce, L. S. (1985). Movement into reading: Is the first stage of printed word learning visual or phonetic? *Reading Research Quarterly, 20,* 163-179.

Gough, P. B., & Hillinger, M. L. (1980). Learning to read: An unnatural act. *Bulletin of the Orton Society, 30,* 180-196.

Mason (1980) op. cit.

37. Martin, B., & Brogan, P. (1971). *Teacher's guide to the instant readers.* New York: Holt, Rinehart, & Winston.

38. Durkin (1966) op. cit.

39. Moore, O. K., & Anderson, A. R. (1968). The responsive environments project. In R. D.

Hess & R. M. Bear (Eds.), *Early education* (pp. 171-189). Chicago, IL: Aldine.

40. A general review of the value of early writing in helping young children refine their understanding of the written language system is provided by Dyson, A. H. (1984). Reading, writing, and language: Young children solving the written language puzzle. In J. M. Jensen (Ed.), *Composing and comprehending* (pp. 165-175). Urbana, IL: National Conference on Research in English and ERIC Clearinghouse on Reading and Communication Skills.

41. Chomsky (1971, 1979) op. cit.

    Read, C. (1971). Pre-school children's knowledge of English phonology. *Harvard Educational Review, 41*, 1-34.

42. Harste, J., Woodward, V. A., & Burke, C. L. (1984). *Language stories and literacy lessons.* Exeter, NH: Heinemann.

43. Educational Products Information Exchange. (1977). *Report on a national study of the nature and the quality of instructional materials most used by teachers and learners* (Tech. Rep. No. 76). New York: EPIE Institute.

    Fisher, C. W., Berliner, D., Filby, N., Marliave, R., Cohen, L., Dishaw, M., & Moore, J. (1978). *Teaching and learning in elementary schools: A summary of the beginning teacher evaluation study.* San Francisco, CA: Far West Regional Laboratory for Educational Research and Development. For a briefer account of this research, see Teaching behaviors, academic learning time, and student achievement: An overview. In C. Denham & A. Lieberman (Eds.). (1980). *Time to learn* (pp. 7-32). Washington, DC: National Institute of Education.

44. Anderson, L. (1984). The environment of instruction: The function of seatwork in a commercially developed curriculum. In G. G. Duffy, L. R. Roehler, & J. Mason (Eds.), *Comprehension instruction: Perspectives and suggestions* (pp. 93-103). New York: Longman.

    Fisher et al. (1978) op. cit.

    Mason, J., & Osborn, J. (1982). *When do children begin "reading to learn"?: A survey of classroom reading instruction practices in grades two through five* (Tech. Rep. No. 261). Urbana: University of Illinois, Center for the Study of Reading.

    Shannon, P. (1983). The use of commercial reading materials in American elementary schools. *Reading Research Quarterly, 19*, 68-85.

45. Perfetti, C. A., & Lesgold, A. M. (1979). Coding and comprehension in skilled reading and implications for reading instruction. In L. B. Resnick & P. A. Weaver (Eds.), *Theory and practice of early reading* (Vol. 1, pp. 57-84). Hillsdale, NJ: Erlbaum.

46. Smith, N. B. (1965). *American reading instruction.* Newark, DE: International Reading Association.

47. Mathews, M. M. (1966). *Teaching to read, historically considered.* Chicago, IL: University of Chicago Press.

48. Flesch, R. (1955). *Why Johnny can't read.* New York: Harper.

49. Chall, J. S. (1967). *Learning to read: The great debate.* New York: McGraw-Hill. In her recent update of the research from the past fifteen years (See Note 50), Chall found even stronger evidence for phonics.

50. Chall, J. S. (1983). *Learning to read: The great debate* (2nd ed.). New York: McGraw-Hill.

    Johnson, D. D., & Baumann, J. F. (1984). Word identification. In P. D. Pearson (Ed.), *Handbook of reading research* (pp. 583-608). New York: Longman.

    Pflaum, S. W., Walberg, H. J., Karegianes, M. L., & Rasher, S. P. (1980). Reading instruction: A quantitative analysis. *Educational Researcher, 9*, 12-18.

    Williams, J. P. (1985). The case for explicit decoding instruction. In J. Osborn, P. T. Wilson, & R. C. Anderson (Eds.), *Reading education: Foundations for a literate America* (pp. 205-213). Lexington, MA: Lexington Books.

51. Becker, W. C., & Gersten, R. (1982). A follow-up of Follow-Through: The later effects of the Direct Instruction model on children in fifth and sixth grades. *American Educational Research Journal, 19*, 75-92. For an examination of the long-term effects of the Direct Instruction model on students in high school, see Meyer, L. A. (1984). Long-term academic effects of the Direct Instruction Project Follow Through. *The Elementary School Journal, 84*, 380-394.

52. Alternative terms which have often been used for explicit and implicit phonics are synthetic and analytic phonics, deductive and inductive phonics, or direct and indirect phonics.

53. The slashes // indicate a speech sound. This is a notation used in the International Phonetic Alphabet. The complete notation system uses other special symbols to precisely identify sounds. In this document, the slashes will be used to indicate a speech sound, but the rest of the symbols will not be employed. When the slashes are used here, the intended sound can be determined from the context.

54. The examples used in text are generic examples that can be found in programs such as the following:

Buchanan, C. D. (1973). *Programmed reading: A Sullivan Associates program* (3rd ed.). New York: McGraw-Hill.

Engelmann, S., & Bruner, E. C. (1974). *Distar reading I: An instructional system* (2nd ed.). Chicago, IL: Science Research Associates.

Hughes, A., Bernier, S. A., Thomas, N., Bereiter, C., Anderson, V., Gurren, L., Lebo, J. D., & Overberg, J. A. (1982). *The Headway program.* La Salle, IL: Open Court.

Matteoni, L., Lane, W. H., Sucher, F., & Yawkey, T. D., Harris, T. L., & Allen, H. B. (1984). *The Keytext program.* Oklahoma City, OK: The Economy Company.

55. See Rosenshine, B., & Stevens, R. (1984). Classroom instruction in reading. In P. D. Pearson (Ed.), *Handbook of reading research* (pp. 745-798). New York: Longman. For an experimental study in which blending facilitates the word recognition performance of kindergarten children, see Haddock, M. (1976). The effects of an auditory and auditory-visual method of blending instruction on the ability of prereaders to decode synthetic words. *Journal of Educational Psychology, 68,* 825-831.

56. Beck, I. L., & McCaslin, E. S. (1978). *An analysis of dimensions that affect the development of code-breaking ability in eight beginning reading programs* (LRDC Publication 1978/6). Pittsburgh, PA: University of Pittsburgh, Learning Research and Development Center.

57. The examples used in text are generic examples that can be found in programs such as the following:

Aaron, I. E., Jackson, D., Riggs, C., Smith, R. G., & Tierney, R. J. (1983). *Scott, Foresman reading.* Glenview, IL: Scott Foresman & Company.

Clymer, T., Venezky, R. L., & Indrisano, R. (1984). *Ginn reading program.* Lexington, MA: Ginn & Company.

Early, M., Cooper, E. K., & Santeusanio, N. (1983). *HBJ Bookmark reading program.* Orlando, FL: Harcourt Brace Jovanovich.

It should be noted that one program that employs an implicit phonics approach does allow the teacher to produce some vowel sounds in isolation. See Durr, W. K., LePere, J. M., Pescosolido, J., Bean, R. M., & Glaser, N. A. (1983). *Houghton Mifflin reading program.* Boston, MA: Houghton Mifflin Company.

58. Durkin, D. (1983). *Is there a match between what elementary teachers do and what basal reader manuals recommend?* (Reading Ed. Rep. No. 44). Urbana: University of Illinois, Center for the Study of Reading. A briefer account of this research is available under the same title in *The Reading Teacher* (1984), *37,* 734-744.

59. E.g.:

Bruce, D. J. (1964). Analysis of word sounds by young children. *British Journal of Educational Psychology, 34,* 158-169.

Calfee, R. C., Chapman, R. S., & Venezky, R. L. (1972). How a child needs to think to learn to read. In L. W. Gregg (Ed.), *Cognition in learning and memory.* New York: Wiley.

Liberman, I. Y. (1973). Segmentation of the spoken word and reading acquisition. *Bulletin of the Orton Society, 23,* 65-77.

Liberman, I. Y., Cooper, F. S., Shankweiler, D., & Studdert-Kennedy, M. (1967). Perception of the speech code. *Psychological Review, 74,* 431-461.

Rosner, J. (1973). Language arts and arithmetic achievement and specifically related perceptual skills. *American Educational Research Journal, 10,* 59-68.

60. Resnick, L. B., & Beck, I. L. (1976). Designing instruction in reading: Interaction of theory and practice. In J. T. Guthrie (Ed.), *Aspects of reading acquisition* (pp. 180-204). Baltimore, MD: Johns Hopkins University Press.

61. Cohen, A. S. (1974-1975). Oral reading errors of first-grade children taught by a code-emphasis approach. *Reading Research Quarterly, 10,* 616-650.

Norton, D. (1976). A comparison of the oral

reading errors of high and low ability first and third graders taught by two approaches — synthetic phonic and analytic-eclectic. (Doctoral dissertation, University of Wisconsin-Madison). *Dissertation Abstracts Inernational, 37,* 3399A.

62. Biemiller, A. (1970). The development of the use of graphic and contextual information as children learn to read. *Reading Research Quarterly, 6,* 75-96.

53. Carnine, L., Carnine, D., & Gersten, R. (1984). Analysis of oral reading errors made by economically disadvantaged students taught with a synthetic-phonics approach. *Reading Research Quarterly, 19,* 343-356.

54. Goodman, K. S. (1976). The reading process: A psycholinguistic view. In E. B. Smith, K. S. Goodman, & R. Meredith. *Language and thinking in school* (pp.265-283). New York: Holt, Rinehart & Winston. Kenneth Goodman also provides pertinent comment on the efficacy of phonics instruction in *Reading: A conversation with Kenneth Goodman.* (1976). Glenview, IL: Scott, Foresman and Company, p.7.

Smith, F. (1973). Decoding: The great fallacy. In F. Smith (Ed.), *Psycholinguistics and reading* (pp. 70-83). New York: Holt, Rinehart & Winston.

5. See Note 50.

6. The advantages of having children identify words by analogy with other known words was first noted by Gates, A. I., & Russell, D. H. (1938). Types of materials, vocabulary burden, word analysis, and other factors in beginning reading. II. *Elementary School Journal, 39,* 119-128. For a recent application of this approach, see Cunningham, P. M. (1975-1976). Investigating a synthesized theory of mediated word identification. *Reading Research Quarterly, 11,* 127-143.

7. To simplify this discussion, "pre-primers" and "first readers" are being included together with primers.

8. For thoughtful discussions of the characteristics of primers, see:

Beck, I. L. (1981). Reading problems and instructional practices. In G. E. MacKinnon & T. G. Waller (Eds.), *Reading research: Advances in theory and practice* (Vol. 2, pp. 53-95). New York: Academic Press.

Willows, D. M., Borwick, D., & Hayvren, M. (1981). The content of school readers. In G. E. MacKinnon & T. G. Waller (Eds.), *Reading research: Advances in theory and practice* (Vol. 2, pp. 97-175). New York: Academic Press.

69. For a description of the informal methods of instruction used in New Zealand, see Clay, M. M. (1976). Early childhood and cultural diversity in New Zealand. *The Reading Teacher, 29,* 333-342. Favorable results seem to have been achieved by these methods, as suggested by recent cross-national studies of reading:

Guthrie, J. (1981). Reading in New Zealand: Achievement and volume. *Reading Research Quarterly, 17,* 6-27.

Purves, A. C. (1973). *Literature education in ten countries: An empirical study.* New York: Wiley.

Thorndike, R. L. (1973). *Reading comprehension education in fifteen countries: An empirical study.* New York: Wiley.

70. Bond & Dykstra (1967) op. cit.

71. From "Mix and make". (1982). In T. Clymer & R. L. Venezky, *Ginn reading program* (Level 3, Unit 2). Lexington, MA: Ginn & Company, pp. 36-37.

72. From "At the seashore". (1982). In A. Hughes, S. A. Bernier, N. Thomas, C. Bereiter, V. Anderson, L. Gurren, J. D. Lebo, & J. A. Overberg. *The Headway program* (Level B-1, Lesson 17). LaSalle, IL: Open Court, p. 67.

73. Beck (1981) op. cit.

74. Ruddell, R. B. (1965). The effect of oral and written patterns of language structure on reading comprehension. *The Reading Teacher, 18,* 270-275.

Tatham, S. M. (1970). Reading comprehension of materials written with select oral language patterns: A study at grades two and four. *Reading Research Quarterly, 3* 402-426.

Wilkinson, I. A. G., & Brown, C. A. (1983). Oral reading strategies of year one children as a function of level of ability and method of instruction. *Reading Psychology, 4,* 1-9.

75. Dr. Seuss. (1960). *Green eggs and ham.* New York: Beginner Press.

76. Mason & Osborn (1982) op. cit.

Shannon (1983) op. cit.

77. Durkin (1983) op. cit.

Mason, J. (1983). An examination of reading instruction in third and fourth grades. *The Reading Teacher, 36,* 906-913.

78. Durkin (1983) op. cit.

    Mason & Osborn (1982) op. cit.

79. E.g:

    Hansen, J. (1981). The effects of inference training and practice on young children's reading comprehension. *Reading Research Quarterly, 16,* 391-417.

    Hansen, J., & Pearson, P. D. (1983). An instructional study: Improving the inferential comprehension of good and poor fourth-grade readers. *Journal of Educational Psychology, 75,* 821-829.

    Omanson, R. C., Beck, I. L., Voss, J. F., & McKeown, M. G. (1984). The effects of reading lessons on comprehension: A processing description. *Cognition and Instruction, 1,* 45-67.

80. Beck, I. L., McCaslin, E. S., & McKeown, M. G. (1981). Basal readers' purpose for story reading: Smoothly paving the road or setting up a detour? *Elementary School Journal, 81,* 156-161.

81. Beck, I. L., Omanson, R. C., & McKeown, M. G. (1982). An instructional redesign of reading lessons: Effects on comprehension. *Reading Research Quarterly, 17,* 462-481.

82. Ibid.

83. Allington, R. L. (1982). *Amount and mode of contextual reading as a function of reading group membership.* Paper presented at the National Council of Teachers of English, Washington, DC.

84. This conclusion is suggested by studies of repeated reading (see Samuels, 1985 op. cit.) and by research described by Brecht, R. D. (1977). Testing format and instructional level with the informal reading inventory. *The Reading Teacher, 31,* 57-59.

85. Durkin (1983) op. cit.

86. Collins, J. (1980). *Differential treatment in reading instruction.* Berkely, CA: Language Behavior Research Laboratory.

87. Anderson, L. M., Evertson, C. M., & Brophy, J. E. (1979). An experimental study of effective teaching in first-grade reading groups. *The Elementary School Journal, 79,* 193-223.

    Hoffman, J. V., O'Neal, S. F., Kastler, L. A., Clements, R. O., Segel, K. W., & Nash, M. F. (1984). Guided oral reading and miscue focused verbal feedback in second-grade classrooms. *Reading Research Quarterly, 19,* 367-384.

88. Anderson, R. C., Mason, J., & Shirey, L. (1984). The reading group: An experimental investigation of a labyrinth. *Reading Research Quarterly, 20,* 6-38.

89. E.g. Anderson, Evertson, & Brophy (1979) op. cit.

90. Dahl, P. R., & Samuels, S. J. (1979). An experimental program for teaching high speed word recognition and comprehension skills. In J. E. Button, T. C. Lovitt, & T. D. Rowland (Eds.), *Communications research in learning disabilities and mental retardation.* Baltimore, MD: University Park Press.

    Herman, P. A. (in press). The effect of repeated readings on reading rate, speech pauses and word recognition accuracy. *Reading Research Quarterly.*

    Samuels (1985) op. cit.

91. Allington, R. L. (1984). Oral reading. In P. D. Pearson (Ed.), *Handbook of reading research* (pp. 829-864). New York: Longman.

    Leinhardt, G., Zigmond, N., & Cooley, W. W. (1981). Reading instruction and its effects. *American Educational Research Journal, 18,* 343-361.

92. See Tharp, R. G. (1982). The effective instruction of comprehension: Results and description of the Kamehameha Early Education Program. *Reading Research Quarterly, 17,* 503-527.

93. Bransford, J. D., Stein, B. S., Vye, N. J., Franks, J. J., Auble, P. M., Mezynski, K. J., & Perfetto, G. A. (1982). Differences in approaches to learning: An overview. *Journal of Experimental Psychology: General, 111,* 390-398. Also see the subsequent three papers by Bransford and his colleagues in this volume.

    Owings, R. A., Peterson, G. A., Bransford, J. D., Morris, C. D., & Stein, B. S. (1980). Spontaneous monitoring and regulation of learning: A comparison of successful and less successful fifth graders. *Journal of Educational Psychology, 72,* 250-256.

    Paris, S. G., & Lindauer, B. K. (1976). The role of inference in children's comprehension and memory for sentences. *Cognitive Psychology, 8,* 217-227.

94. Beck, Omanson, & McKeown (1982) op. cit.

    Hansen (1981) op. cit.

    Hansen & Pearson (1983) op. cit.

95. Durkin (1983) op. cit.

96. Beck, I. L., & McKeown, M. G. (1981). Developing questions that promote comprehension: The story map. *Language Arts, 58,* 913-918.

97. See Duffy, G. G. (1981). Teacher effectiveness research: Implications for the reading profession. In M. L. Kamil (Ed.), *Directions in reading: Research and instruction* (pp. 113-136). Washington, DC: National Reading Conference.

98. Rosenshine & Stevens (1984) op. cit.

Extending Literacy

1. Hirsch, E. D., Jr. (1983). Cultural literacy. *The American Scholar, 53,* 159-169.

2. Fry, E. B. (1968). A readability formula that saves time. *The Journal of Reading, 11,* 513-516; 575-578.

3. Chall, J. S. (1958). *Readability: An appraisal of research and application.* Columbus, OH: Ohio State University.

   Klare, G. R. (1984). Readability. In P. D. Pearson (Ed.), *Handbook of reading research* (pp. 681-744). New York: Longman.

4. Klare (1984) op. cit. pp. 717-718.

5. Chall, J. S. (1984). Readability and prose comprehension: continuities and discontinuities. In J. Flood (Ed.), *Understanding reading comprehension: Cognition, language and the structure of prose.* Newark, DE: International Reading Association.

   Davison, A. (1984). Readability — appraising text difficulty. In R. C. Anderson, J. Osborn, & R. J. Tierney (Eds.), *Learning to read in American schools: Basal readers and content texts* (pp. 121-139). Hillsdale, NJ: Erlbaum.

6. The rewritten version is from "Little Hippo". (1980). In W. Eller, K. B. Hester et al. *The Laidlaw reading program* (Level 6, Reader 1). River Forest, IL: Laidlaw Brothers, p. 46. It was adapted from the original by Bennett, R. (1960). *The secret hiding place.* Cleveland, OH: World, p. 1.

7. Ibid. pp. 48 and 3 respectively.

8. Applebee, A. N. (1980). Children's narratives: New directions. *The Reading Teacher, 34,* 137-142.

   Stein, N. L., & Trabasso, T. (1982). What's in a story: An approach to comprehension and instruction. In R. Glaser (Ed.), *Advances in instructional psychology* (Vol. 2, pp. 213-254). Hillsdale, NJ: Erlbaum.

9. Stein & Trabasso (1982) op. cit.

10. Beck, I. L., McKeown, M. G., & McCaslin, E. S. (1981). Does reading make sense? Problems of early readers. *The Reading Teacher, 34,* 780-785.

    Stein & Trabasso (1982) op. cit.

11. Bruce, B. C. (1984). A new point of view on children's stories. In R. C. Anderson, J. Osborn, & R. J. Tierney (Eds.), *Learning to read in American schools: Basal readers and content texts* (pp. 153-174). Hillsdale, NJ: Erlbaum.

    Steinberg, C., & Bruce, B. C. (1980). *Higher-level features in children's stories: Rhetorical structure and conflict* (Reading Ed. Rep. No. 18). Urbana: University of Illinois, Center for the Study of Reading.

    Willows, D. M., Borwick, D., & Hayvren, M. (1981). The content of school readers. In G. E. MacKinnon & T. G. Waller (Eds.), *Reading research: Advances in theory practice* (Vol. 2, pp. 97-175). New York: Academic Press.

12. From "The raccoon and Mrs. McGinnis". (1976). In T. Clymer & P. M. Martin, *Reading 720* (Level 7, Unit 6). Lexington, MA: Ginn & Company, p. 234.

13. Beck, I. L., McKeown, M. G., Omanson, R. C., & Pople, M. T. (1984). Improving the comprehensibility of stories: The effects of revisions that improve coherence. *Reading Research Quarterly, 19,* 263-277.

14. Blom, G. E., Waite, R. W., & Zimet, S. G. (1970). A motivational content analysis of children's primers. In H. Levin & J. P. Williams (Eds.), *Basic studies on reading* (pp. 188-221). New York: Basic Books.

    Bruce (1984) op. cit.

    Chall, J. S., Conrad, S. S., and Harris, S. H. (1977). *An analysis of textbooks in relation to declining SAT scores.* New York: College Entrance Examination Board.

    Chall, J. S., Conrad, S. S., and Harris-Sharples, S. H. (1983). *Textbooks and challenge: An inquiry into textbook difficulty, reading achievement, and knowledge acquisition.* Final report to the Spencer Foundation.

15. Gallagher, M. C., & Pearson, P. D. (1982). *An examination of expository texts in elementary instructional materials.* Paper presented at the National Reading Conference, Clearwater, FL.

    Gallagher, M. C., & Pearson, P. D. (1983). *Fourth grade students' acquisition of new information from text.* Paper presented at the National Reading Conference, Austin, TX.

16. Bartlett, B. J. (1978). *Top-level structure as an organizational strategy for recall of classroom text.* Unpublished doctoral dissertation, Arizona State University.

    Meyer, B. J. F., Brandt, D. M., & Bluth, G. J. (1980). Use of top-level structure in text: Key for reading comprehension of ninth-grade students. *Reading Research Quarterly, 16,* 72-103.

17. The classic reference on this point is Bruner, J. (1960). *The process of education.* Cambridge, MA: Harvard University Press.

18. Anderson, T. H., & Armbruster, B. B. (1984). Content area textbooks. In R. C. Anderson, J. Osborn, & R. J. Tierney (Eds.), *Learning to read in American schools: Basal readers and content texts* (pp. 193-226). Hillsdale, NJ: Erlbaum.

    Armbruster, B. B. (1984). The problem of "inconsiderate text". In G. G. Duffy, L. R. Roehler, & J. Mason (Eds.), *Comprehension instruction: Perspectives and suggestions* (pp. 202-217). New York: Longman.

19. This example is described in Armbruster, B. B., & Anderson, T. H. (1984). Structures of explanations in history textbooks or so what if Governor Stanford missed the spike and hit the rail? *Journal of Curriculum Studies, 16,* 181-194.

20. Ibid.

21. Herman, P. A. (1984, December). *Incidental learning of word meanings from expository texts that systematically vary text features.* Paper presented at the National Reading Conference, St. Petersburg, FL.

22. The rewritten version is from Herman, P. A. (in preparation). *Incidental learning of word meanings from expository texts that systematically vary text features.* Unpublished doctoral dis-

    sertation, University of Illinois. It was adapted from the original "Circulation, respiration, and excretion". (1977). In C. Heimler & J. Lockard. *Life science* (pp. 272-280). Columbus, OH: Charles Merrill Publishing, p. 273.

23. Herman (1984, December) op. cit.

24. See, for example:

    Baumann, J. F. (1984). The effectiveness of a direct instruction paradigm for teaching main idea comprehension. *Reading Research Quarterly, 20,* 93-115.

    Patching, W., Kameenui, E., Carnine, D., Gersten, R., & Colvin, G. (1983). Direct instruction in critical reading skills. *Reading Research Quarterly, 18,* 406-418.

    Palincsar, A. S., & Brown, A. L. (1984). Reciprocal teaching of comprehension-fostering and comprehension-monitoring activities. *Cognition and Instruction, 1,* 117-175.

    Paris, S. G., Cross, D. R., & Lipson, M. Y. (1984). Informed strategies for learning: A program to improve children's reading awareness and comprehension. *Journal of Educational Psychology, 76,* 1239-1252.

25. See Paris, S. G. (in press). Teaching children to guide their reading and learning. In T. E. Raphael & R. Reynolds (Eds.), *Contexts of literacy.* New York: Longman.

26. Duffy, G. G. (1981). Teacher effectiveness research: Implications for the reading profession. In M. L. Kamil (Ed.), *Directions in reading: Research and instruction* (pp. 113-136). Washington, DC: National Reading Conference.

27. Palincsar & Brown (1984) op. cit.

28. Paris, Cross, & Lipson (1984) op. cit.

29. Durkin, D. (1978-1979). What classroom observations reveal about reading comprehension instruction. *Reading Research Quarterly, 14,* 481-533.

    Neilsen, A. R., Rennie, B. J., & Connell, A. M. (1982). Allocation of instructional time to reading comprehension and study skills in intermediate grade social studies classrooms. In J. A. Niles & L. A. Harris (Eds.), *New inquiries in reading research and instruction* (pp. 81-84). Rochester, NY: National Reading Conference.

30. Durkin (1978-1979) op. cit.

31. Hare, V. C., & Milligan, B. (1984). **Main idea**

identification: Instructional explanations in four basal reader series. *Journal of Reading Behavior, 16,* 189-204.

32. Fisher, C. W., Berliner, D., Filby, N., Marliave, R., Cohen, L., Dishaw, M., & Moore, J. (1978). *Teaching and learning in elementary schools: A summary of the beginning teacher evaluation study.* San Francisco, CA: Far West Regional Laboratory for Educational Research and Development. For a briefer account of this research, see Teaching behaviors, academic learning time, and student achievement: An overview. In C. Denham & A. Lieberman (Eds.). (1980). *Time to learn* (pp. 7-32). Washington, DC: National Institute of Education.

33. Osborn, J. (1984). The purposes, uses, and contents of workbooks and some guidelines for publishers. In R. C. Anderson, J. Osborn, & R. J. Tierney (Eds.), *Learning to read in American schools: Basal readers and content texts* (pp. 45-111). Hillsdale, NJ: Erlbaum.

Osborn, J. (1985). Workbooks: Counting, matching, and judging. In J. Osborn, P. T. Wilson, & R. C. Anderson, (Eds.), *Reading education: Foundations for a literate America* (pp. 11-28). Lexington, MA: Lexington Books.

34. This example is described in Osborn, J. (1984). *Evaluating workbooks* (Reading Ed. Rep. No. 52). Urbana: University of Illinois, Center for the Study of Reading, p. 23.

35. Anderson, L. (1984). The environment of instruction: The function of seatwork in a commercially developed curriculum. In G. G. Duffy, L. R. Roehler, & J. Mason (Eds.), *Comprehension instruction: Perspectives and suggestions* (pp. 93-103). New York: Longman.

36. This conclusion is suggested by the research described in:

Leinhardt, G., Zigmond, N., & Cooley, W. W. (1981). Reading instruction and its effects. *American Educational Research Journal, 18,* 343-361.

Rosenshine, B., & Stevens, R. (1984). Classroom instruction in reading. In P. D. Pearson (Ed.), *Handbook of reading research* (pp. 745-798). New York: Longman.

37. Allington, R. L. (1984) Oral reading. In P. D. Pearson (Ed.), *Handbook of reading research* (pp. 829-864). New York: Longman.

Elley, W. B., & Mangubhai, F. (1983). The impact of reading on second language learning. *Reading Research Quarterly, 19,* 53-67.

Ingham, J. (1981). *Books and reading development.* London: Heinemann.

Leinhardt, Zigmond, & Cooley (1981) op. cit.

38. Dishaw, M. (1977). *Descriptions of allocated time to content areas for the A-B period* (Beginning Teacher Evaluation Study Tech. Note IV-11a). San Francisco, CA: Far West Regional Laboratory for Educational Research and Development.

39. Fielding, L. G., Wilson, P. T., & Anderson, R. C. (in press). A new focus on free reading: The role of trade books in reading instruction. In T. E. Raphael & R. Reynolds (Eds.), *Contexts of literacy.* New York: Longman.

Greany, V. (1980). Factors related to amount and type of leisure time reading. *Reading Research Quarterly, 15,* 337-357.

Heyns, B. (1978). *Summer learning and the effects of schooling.* New York: Academic Press.

Walberg, H. J., & Tsai, S. (1984). Reading achievement and diminishing returns to time. *Journal of Educational Psychology, 76,* 442-451.

40. Fielding, Wilson, & Anderson (in press) op. cit.

41. Fielding, Wilson, & Anderson (in press) op. cit.

42. Nagy, W. E., Herman, P. A., & Anderson, R. C. (1985). Learning words from context. *Reading Research Quarterly, 20,* 233-253.

43. Ibid.

44. Fielding, Wilson, & Anderson (in press) op. cit.

45. Fielding, Wilson, & Anderson (in press) op. cit.

46. Heyns (1978) op. cit.

47. Statistics quoted to this point in the paragraph are from Heintze, R. A., & Hodes, L. (1981). *Statistics of public school libraries/media centers 1978 Fall.* Washington DC: National Center for Education Statistics.

48. Libraries and the Learning Society. (1984). *Alliance for excellence: Librarians respond to A Nation at Risk.* Washington, DC: U.S. Department of Education, p. 14.

49. Elley & Mangubhai (1983) op. cit.

Ingham (1981) op. cit.

50. Elley & Mangubhai (1983) op. cit.

51. Fielding, Wilson, & Anderson (in press) op.

cit.

Ingham (1981) op. cit.

52. For a comprehensive review of the literature in this area, see Tierney, R. J., & Leys, M. (in press). What is the value of connecting reading and writing? In B. Peterson (Ed.), *Convergences: Essays on reading, writing, and literacy.* Urbana, IL: National Council of Teachers of English.

53. From Calkins, L. (1983). *Lessons from a child.* Exeter, NH: Heinemann, p. 157.

54. Bridge, C. A., & Hiebert, E. H. (in press). A comparison of classroom writing practices, teachers' perceptions of their writing instructions, and textbook recommendations on writing practices. *Elementary School Journal.*

55. Applebee, A. N. (1981). *Writing in the secondary school.* Urbana, IL: National Council of Teachers of English.

56. See Braddock, R., Lloyd-Jones, R., & Schoer, L. (1963). *Research in written composition.* Urbana, IL: National Council of Teachers of English. For pertinent comment on the role of formal grammar instruction in helping students learn how to use language for communicative purposes, see Postman, N. (1967). Linguistics and the pursuit of relevance. *English Journal, 56,* 1160-1165.

57. This conclusion is suggested by the research desribed in:

Calkins, L. M. (1980, May). When children want to punctuate: Basic skills belong in context. *Language Arts, 57,* 567-573.

Graves, D. H. (1982). *A case study observing the development of primary children's composing, spelling, and motor behaviors during the writing process* (Final Report Project No. 8-3419-0963). Washington, DC: National Institute of Education.

58. Staton, J., Shuy, R., & Kreeft, J. (1982). *Analysis of dialogue journal writing as a communicative event, Volumes I and II.* (NIE-G-80-0122). Final report to the National Institute of Education.

The Teacher and the Classroom

1. These studies are reviewed by Rosenshine, B., & Stevens, R. (1984). Classroom instruction in reading. In P. D. Pearson (Ed.), *Handbook of reading research.* (pp. 745-798). New York: Longman.

2. Lohnes, P. R., & Gray, M. M. (1972). Intellectual development and the Cooperative Reading Studies. *Reading Research Quarterly, 8,* 52-61.

3. Rosenshine & Stevens (1984) op. cit.

4. Rosenshine & Stevens (1984) op. cit.

5. Dishaw, M. (1977). *Descriptions of allocated time to content areas for the A-B period* (Beginning Teacher Evaluation Study Tech. Note IV-11a). San Francisco, CA: Far West Regional Laboratory for Educational Research and Development.

6. Brophy, J. E., & Good, T. L. (in press). Teacher behavior and student achievement. In M. C. Wittrock (Ed.), *Handbook of research on teaching* (3rd ed.). New York: Macmillan.

Rosenshine & Stevens (1984) op. cit.

7. Brophy, J. E. (1983). Classroom organization and management. *Elementary School Journal, 83,* 265-285.

Doyle, W. (in press). Classroom organization and management. In M. C. Wittrock (Ed.), *Handbook of research on teaching* (3rd ed.). New York: Macmillan.

8. Ibid.

9. Brophy, J. E., & Evertson, C. M. (1976). *Learning from teachers: A developmental perspective.* Boston, MA: Allyn and Bacon.

10. Barr, R., & Dreeben, R. (1983). *How schools work.* Chicago, IL: University of Chicago Press.

11. Allington, R. (1984). Content coverage and contextual reading in reading groups. *Journal of Reading Behavior, 16,* 85-96. A similar pattern of results has been reported by Gambrell, L. B. (1984). How much time do children spend reading during teacher-directed reading instruction? In J. A. Niles & L. A. Harris (Eds.), *Changing perspectives on research in reading/language processing and instruction* (pp. 193-198). Rochester, NY: National Reading Conference.

12. See Rosenshine & Stevens (1984) op. cit.

13. Kulik, C. C., & Kulik, J. A. (1982). Effects of ability grouping on secondary school students: A meta-analysis of evaluation findings. *American Educational Research Journal, 19,* 415-428.

14. This conclusion is suggested by research de-

scribed in Cazden, C. B. (1979). Learning to read in classroom interaction. In L. B. Resnick & P. A. Weaver (Eds.), *Theory and practice of early reading* (Vol. 3, pp. 295-306). Hillsdale, NJ: Erlbaum

15. Hiebert, E. H. (1983). An examination of ability grouping for reading instruction. *Reading Research Quarterly, 18,* 231-255.

16. Eder, D., & Felmlee, D. (1984). The development of attention norms in ability groups. In P. Peterson, L. Wilkinson, & N. Hallinan (Eds.), *The social context of instruction* (pp. 189-208). Orlando, FL: Academic Press.

17. McDermott, R. P. (1976). *Kids make sense: An ethnographic account of the interactional management of success and failure in one first-grade classroom.* Unpublished doctoral dissertation, Stanford University.

18. Hiebert (1983) op. cit.

19. Allington, R. L. (1983). The reading instruction provided readers of differing ability. *Elementary School Journal, 83,* 255-265.

   Weinstein, R. S. (in press). The teaching of reading and children's awareness of teacher expectations. In T. E. Raphael & R. Reynolds (Eds.), *Contexts of literacy.* New York: Longman.

20. Hiebert (1983) op. cit.

21. Anderson, R. C., Shirey, L. L., Wilson, P. T., & Fielding, L. G. (in press). Interestingness of children's reading material. In R. E. Snow & M. J. Farr (Eds.), *Aptitude, learning, and instruction: Conative and affective process analyses.* Hillsdale, NJ: Erlbaum.

22. E.g:

   Engelmann, S., & Bruner, E. C. (1974). *Distar reading I, II: An instructional system* (2nd ed.). Chicago, IL: Science Research Associates.

   Hughes, A., Bernier, S. A., Thomas, N., Bereiter, C., Anderson, V., Gurren, L., Lebo, J. D., & Overberg, J. A. (1982). *The Headway program.* La Salle, IL: Open Court.

23. See:

   Glass, G. V. (1984). *The effectiveness of four educational interventions* (Project Rep. No. 84-A19). Stanford, CA: Stanford University, Institute for Research on Educational Finance and Governance.

   Slavin, R. E. (1984). Team Assisted Individualization: Cooperative learning and individualized instruction in the mainstreamed classroom. *Remedial and Special Education, 5,* 33-42.

   Slavin, R. E., & Karweit, N. L. (1984). Mastery learning and student teams: A factorial experiment in urban general mathematics classes. *American Educational Research Journal, 21,* 725-736

Testing and Reading

1. Salmon-Cox, L. (1981). Teachers and standardized achievement tests: What's really happening? *Phi Delta Kappan, 62,* 631-634.

2. Resnick, D. P. (1981). Testing in America: A supportive environment. *Phi Delta Kappan, 62,* 625-628.

3. The classic paper on this distinction is Glaser, R. (1963). Instructional technology and the measurement of learning outcomes: Some questions. *American Psychologist, 18,* 519-521.

4. Block, J., & Anderson, L. W. (1975). *Mastery learning in classroom instruction.* New York: Macmillan.

   Pflaum, S. W., Walberg, H. J., Karegianes, M. L., & Rasher, S. P. (1980). Reading instruction: A quantitative analysis. *Educational Researcher, 9,* 12-18.

5. Johnston, P. H. (1983). *Reading comprehension assessment: A cognitive basis.* Newark, DE: International Reading Association.

   Johnston, P. H. (1984). Prior knowledge and reading comprehension test bias. *Reading Research Quarterly, 19,* 219-239.

6. Johnston (1983) op. cit.

7. Sproull, L., & Zubrow, D. (1981). Standardized testing from the administrative perspective. *Phi Delta Kappan, 62,* 628-631.

   Salmon-Cox (1981) op. cit.

8. Salmon-Cox (1981) op. cit.

9. Edmonds, R. (1985). Characteristics of effective schools: Research and implementation. In J. Osborn, P. T. Wilson, & R. C. Anderson (Eds.), *Reading education: Foundations for a literate America* (pp. 123-130). Lexington, MA: Lexington Books.

   Purkey, S. C., & Smith, M. S. (1983). Effective schools: A review. *Elementary School Journal, 83,* 427-452.

   Rutter, M. (1983). School effects on pupil

progress: Research findings and policy implications. In L. S. Shulman & G. Sykes (Eds.), *Handbook of teaching and policy* (pp. 3-41). New York: Longman.

Weber, G. (1971). *Inner-city children can be taught to read: Four successful schools.* Washington, DC: Council for Basic Education.

10. An argument in support of this is provided by Frederiksen, N. (1984). The real test bias: Influences of testing on teaching and learning. *American Psychologist, 39,* 193-202.

Teacher Education and Professional Development

1. Levin, H. M. (1970). A cost-effective analysis of teacher selection. *Journal of Human Resources, 1,* 24-33.

   Murnane, R. J., & Phillips, B. R. (1978). *Effective teachers of inner-city children: Who they are and what they do.* Princeton, NJ: Mathematica Policy Research.

   Summers, A. A., & Wolfe, B. L. (1977). Do schools make a difference?. *American Economic Review, 67,* 639-652.

2. Kerr, D. H. (1983). Teaching competence and teacher education in the United States. In L. S. Shulman & G. Sykes (Eds.), *Handbook of teaching and policy* (pp. 126-149). New York: Longman.

   Schlechty, P. C., & Vance, V. S. (1981, October). Do academically able teachers leave education?: The North Carolina case. *Phi Delta Kappan, 63,* 106-112.

   Vance, V. S., & Schlechty, P. C. (1982, September). The distribution of academic ability in the teaching force: Policy implications. *Phi Delta Kappan, 64,* 22-27.

3. Personal communication from Dr. Walter W. McMahon, Professor of Economics and Professor of Education, University of Illinois at Urbana-Champaign, January 18, 1985.

   Shanker, A. (1985, January). The revolution that's overdue. *Phi Delta Kappan, 66,* 311-315.

4. Freedman, S., Jackson, J., & Boles, K. (1983). Teaching: An imperilled "profession". In L. S. Shulman & G. Sykes (Eds.), *Handbook of teaching and policy* (pp. 261-299). New York: Longman.

   Lanier, J. E. (in press). Research on teacher education. In M. C. Wittrock (Ed.), *Handbook of research on teaching* (3rd ed.). New York: Macmillan.

5. See Lortie, D. C. (1975). *Schoolteacher: A sociological study.* Chicago, IL: University of Chicago.

6. Ibid.

   Rosenholtz, S. J. (1985, January). Political myths about education reform: Lessons from research on teaching. *Phi Delta Kappan, 66,* 349-355.

7. From Lightfoot, S. L. (1983). The lives of teachers. In L. S. Shulman & G. Sykes (Eds.), *Handbook of teaching and policy* (pp. 241-260). New York: Longman, pp. 241-242.

8. Lanier (in press) op. cit.

9. See Lanier (in press) op. cit.

10. A similar argument is presented by Joyce, B., & Clift, R. (1984). The Phoenix agenda: Essential reform in teacher education. *Educational Researcher, 13,* 5-18.

11. From Nemser, S. F. (1983). Learning to teach. In L. S. Shulman & G. Sykes (Eds.), *Handbook of teaching and policy* (pp. 150-170). New York: Longman, p. 156.

12. See, for example, Acheson, K. A. (1974). *The effects of two microteaching variations: Written versus videotape modeling and audiotape versus videotape feedback.* Paper presented at the American Educational Research Association, Chicago, IL.

13. McMahon, W. W., & Wagner, A. P. (1982). The monetary returns to education as partial social efficiency criteria. In W. W. McMahon & T. G. Geske (Eds.), *Financing education: Overcoming inefficiency and inequity* (pp. 150-187). Urbana: University of Illinois Press.

14. Conant, J. B. (1963). *The education of American teachers.* New York: McGraw-Hill.

15. Grant, C., & Zeichner, K. (1981). Inservice support for first year teachers: The state of the scene. *Journal of Research and Development in Education, 14,* 99-111.

16. From National Institute of Education. (1978). *Beginning teachers and internship programs* (R.F.P. No. 78-0014). Washington, D.C.: National Institute of Education, p. 3.

17. See Waters, C. M., & Wyatt, T. L. (1985, January). Toledo's internship: The teachers'

role in excellence. *Phi Delta Kappan, 66*, 365-367.

18. Remarks of Professor Lee. S. Shulman, Stanford University. Reported in "It's harder to teach in class than to be physician". (1984, Autumn). *The Stanford Educator, School of Education News*, p.3.

19. See Rosenholtz (1985, January) op. cit.

20. Purkey, S. C., & Smith, M. S. (1983). Effective schools: A review. *The Elementary School Journal, 83*, 427-452.

21. Anderson, L. M., Evertson, C. M., & Brophy, J. E. (1979). An experimental study of effective teaching in first-grade reading groups. *The Elementary School Journal, 79*, 193-223.

22. See Coladarci, T., & Gage, N. L. (1984). Effects of a minimal intervention on teacher behavior and student achievement. *American Educational Research Journal, 21*, 539-555.

23. Rutter, M. (1983). School effects on pupil progress: Research findings and policy implications. In L. S. Shulman & G. Sykes (Eds.), *Handbook of teaching and policy* (pp. 3-41). New York: Longman.

24. See Purkey & Smith (1983) op. cit.

25. The account of characteristics of effective schools in this document is based on:

   Purkey & Smith (1983) op. cit.

Rutter (1983) op. cit.

Samuels, S. J. (1981). Characteristics of exemplary reading programs. In J. T. Guthrie (Ed.), *Comprehension and teaching: Research reviews* (pp. 255-273). Newark, DE: International Reading Association.

Venezky, R. L., & Winfield, L. (1979). *Schools that succeed beyond expectations in teaching reading* (Tech. Rep. No. 1). Newark: University of Delaware, Studies on Education.

Afterword

1. Chall, J. S., & Mirsky, A. W. (Eds.). (1978). *Education and the brain.* 77th Year Book of the National Society for the Study of Education, Part II. Chicago, IL: University of Chicago Press.

   Chall, J. S., & Peterson, R. W. (in press). The influence of neuroscience upon educational practice. In S. Friedman & R. W. Peterson (Eds.), *The brain, cognition, and education.* New York: Academic Press.

2. Chall, J. S., & Snow, C. et al. (1982). *Families and literacy.* Final report to the National Institute of Education.

3. See Chall, J. S. (1983). *Stages of reading development.* New York: McGraw-Hill.

Consultants

Marilyn Adams
Researcher
Bolt, Beranek and Newman, Inc.
Cambridge, MA 02238

Virginia Alhorn
Reading Specialist
Tilton School
Danville, Il 61832

Mary Ansaldo
Editor
Ginn & Company
Lexington, MA 02173

Helen Bacon
Professor
Department of Education
University of California
Davis, CA 95616

Marolyn Banner
Reading Specialist
Prairie School
Urbana, IL 61801

Courtney Cazden
Professor
School of Education
Harvard University
Cambridge, MA 02138

Bernice Cullinan
President
International Reading Association
Newark, DE 19711

Alice Davison
Professor
Center for the Study of Reading
University of Illinois
Champaign, IL 61820

Mary Dickinson
First Grade Teacher
Washington School
Champaign, IL 61820

Gerry Duffy
Professor
College of Education
Michigan State University
East Lansing, MI 48824

Dolores Durkin
Professor
Center for the Study of Reading
University of Illinois
Champaign, IL 61820

Linnea Ehri
Professor
Department of Education
University of California
Davis, CA 95616

Jerome Harste
Professor
College of Education
Indiana University
Bloomigton, IN 47401

Carol Helwig
Professor
Elementary and Jr. High Education
Eastern Illinois University
Charleston, IL 61920

Brenda Lerner
Coordinator
Office of School Relations
University of Illinois
Champaign, IL 61820

Patricia Lewis
Fifth Grade Teacher
Robeson School
Champaign, IL 61820

Mitch Ludwinski
Director
Reading Laboratory
Urbana High School
Urbana, IL 61801

Jana Mason
Professor
Center for the Study of Reading
University of Illinois
Champaign, IL 61820

Pat Maxwell
Reading Coordinator
Monticello Public Schools
Monticello, IL 61856

144

Roxanne McClean
Editor
Scott Foresman
Glenview, IL 60025

George McConkie
Professor
Center for the Study of Reading
University of Illinois
Champaign, IL 61820

Linda Meyer
Professor
Center for the Study of Reading
University of Illinois
Champaign, IL 61820

Grace Nunn
Professor
Elementary and Jr. High Education
Eastern Illinois University
Charleston, IL 61920

Andrew Ortony
Professor
Center for the Study of Reading
University of Illinois
Champaign, IL 61820

Jean Osborn
Associate Director
Center for the Study of Reading
University of Illinois
Champaign, IL 61820

David Pearson
Professor
Center for the Study of Reading
University of Illinois
Champaign, IL 61820

Kathryn Ransom
Coordinator of Reading
Springfield Public Schools
Springfield, IL 62704

Robert Reeve
Professor
Center for the Study of Reading
University of Illinois
Champaign, IL 61820

Andee Rubin
Researcher
Bolt, Beranek and Newman, Inc.
Cambridge, MA 02238

Mary Ellen Sronce
Curriculum Coordinator
Urbana School District #116
Urbana, IL 61801

Alice May Swanson
Special Reading Teacher
Rantoul City School District #137
Rantoul, IL 61866

Robert Tierney
Professor
Center for the Study of Reading
University of Illinois
Champaign, IL 61820

Richard Venezky
Professor
Department of Educational Studies
University of Delaware
Newark, DE 19711

Phyllis Wilken
Principal
Garden Hills School
Champaign, IL 61821

Jackie Ziff
Teacher, Grades 5-6
Leal School
Urbana, IL 61801

National Academy of Education

Commission on Education and Public Policy

Co-Chairmen:

Michael Kirst, Professor of Education, Stanford University

Diane Ravitch, Adjunct Associate Professor of History and Education, Teachers College, Columbia University

Members:

Richard C. Atkinson, Chancellor, University of California at San Diego

James S. Coleman, Professor of Sociology, University of Chicago

Lawrence A. Cremin, Frederick A. P. Barnard Professor of Education, President, Teachers College, Columbia University

John W. Gardner, Chairman, Independent Sector, Common Cause

Robert Glaser, University Professor of Psychology and Education, Co-Director, Learning Research and Development Center, University of Pittsburgh

Edmund W. Gordon, Professor of Psychology, Yale University

Patricia A. Graham, Charles Warren Professor of History of Education, Harvard University

Thomas F. Green, Margaret Slocum Professor of Education, Syracuse University

H. Thomas James, President, The Spencer Foundation

Lee S. Shulman, Professor of Education, Stanford University

Martin Trow, Professor of Public Policy, Director of the Center for Studies in Higher Education, University of California at Berkeley

National Academy of Education

How to Order

School districts, governmental agencies and other organizations in the U.S. may use a purchase order for orders of 10 books or more. All purchase orders are subject to credit approval and **purchase orders will not be filled without a Federal Employee Identification Number.**

Individuals must prepay all orders.

Each order of 50 books (one box) receives a 33 ⅓ % discount. (Boxes of 50 cannot be broken at this discount price.) Quantities less than 50 are sold at the per copy price.

Please note: For prepaid orders, prices include library rate or 4th class postage and handling. For purchase orders, shipping and handling will be billed. Prices are subject to change without notice. Foreign checks must have the name of a United States correspondent bank imprinted or they will be returned.

**All sales are final, except
for defective copies**

For further information, please call the Center for the Study of Reading at (217) 333-7647.

- -

Name _____

Address _____

_____

_____

Phone # _____

Single copies **(up to 50)**_____ at $4.50 per copy $_____
Boxes **(of 50 copies)**_____ at $150.00 per box $_____
Add Sales Tax:
IL-6¼%   OH-5%
WI-5%   IN-5%
MN-6%   MI-4% $_____
Overseas mailing add $1.00 per copy $_____
Total amount $_____

Method of payment

( )   Our purchase order (for 10 books or more) is enclosed. Our Federal Employer Identification Number is_____

( )   My personal check or money order is enclosed.

Make check, purchase order, or money order payable to:

University of Illinois — BNR

Mail orders to: **Becoming a Nation of Readers
P.O. Box 2774, Station A
Champaign, IL 61820-8774**